Jesus had an intentional strategy for mak
Jesus, Peter Roennfeldt takes us on a remarkable and insightful journey through the life of Jesus, revealing the essential components of His disciplemaking strategy. You will discover that this process was simple, relational, and reproducible. Having had Dr. Roennfeldt as a tour guide in Israel and attending numerous seminars by him on this theme over the years, I know that this practical study guide will inspire, equip, challenge, and encourage every follower of Jesus to be a disciplemaker. Whether you use this material devotionally or as part of a small group, seminar, or sermon series, you will see the need to make discipleship the basic operating system of the church once again.

SIMON MARTIN, church growth and mission director, south England

Many have decided to follow Jesus, but not many are able to describe how they were discipled. Only a few have been trained to disciple others. *Following Jesus* is one of the most comprehensive resources to help individuals and groups study the life of Jesus in a way that leads to a true learning experience in discipleship. We have translated this material into Finnish, and many community Bible-reading groups have been using it in Finland. The feedback has been very positive.

ATTE HELMINEN, city pastor and coach, Helsinki, Finland

In this era of ever-increasing complexity, it is refreshing to be held at the feet of Jesus, listening to His words. Like Martha of old, we are prone to get busy doing all the things we think are necessary to serve Him, but Mary was commended by Jesus for her choice to sit at His feet and listen. Peter has provided a tool to assist us to do just that with the focus on the person, passion, and missional purpose of Jesus. I highly recommend this as a journey for all who seek to follow Jesus as their model in life and ministry.

BILL HODGSON, Power to Change—church movements, SHIFTm2M

FOLLOWING JESUS

A YEAR OF DISCIPLEMAKING AND
MOVEMENT BUILDING IN THE GOSPELS

PETER ROENNFELDT

A NavPress resource published in alliance
with Tyndale House Publishers

NavPress is the publishing ministry of The Navigators, an international Christian organization and leader in personal spiritual development. NavPress is committed to helping people grow spiritually and enjoy lives of meaning and hope through personal and group resources that are biblically rooted, culturally relevant, and highly practical.

For more information, visit NavPress.com.

Following Jesus: A Year of Disciplemaking and Movement Building in the Gospels

Copyright © 2022 by Peter Roennfeldt. All rights reserved.

Published in North America by permission of Signs Publishing, Warburton, VIC, Australia, copyright © 2018 by Peter Roennfeldt. First printed, 2017.

A NavPress resource published in alliance with Tyndale House Publishers

NavPress and the NavPress logo are registered trademarks of NavPress, The Navigators, Colorado Springs, CO. *Tyndale* is a registered trademark of Tyndale House Ministries. Absence of ® in connection with marks of NavPress or other parties does not indicate an absence of registration of those marks.

The Team:

David Zimmerman, Publisher; Deborah Gonzalez, Development Editor; Elizabeth Schroll, Copy Editor; Olivia Eldredge, Operations Manager; Lindsey Bergsma, Designer

Cover design and illustration by Lindsey Bergsma. Copyright © Tyndale House Ministries. All rights reserved.

Author photo copyright © 2019 by Peter Roennfeldt. All rights reserved.

For information about special discounts for bulk purchases, please contact Tyndale House Publishers at csresponse@tyndale.com, or call 1-855-277-9400.

ISBN 978-1-64158-511-8

Printed in the United States of America

28 27 26 25 24 23 22
7   6   5   4   3   2   1

To my family:

Judy, David and Maryanne, Troy and Cindi, and

grandchildren—Inez, Finn, Kai, and Eva.

Just like you can't live without water,
Man can't live without God.

Rodney Onchera
10/13/22

CONTENTS

FOREWORD

FOLLOWING JESUS is what every person influenced by Jesus Christ is challenged to do. For some, it seems to come naturally, but for others, there is a tendency to stagnation, becoming a passive believer. All of us who are enthralled by Jesus want to be all we can be as genuine followers. But the questions remain: *How can I be a real follower of Jesus? How long will it take?*

In this book, Peter Roennfeldt uses the story of Jesus in the Gospels to show the intentional journey that He took His original followers on. There were clear steps in His plan, and He was patient. His disciples followed, fell back, got up, and moved on again. In *Following Jesus*, we are invited on the journey into discipleship that Jesus led His first disciples on. We will read the book and the Gospels, reflect and perhaps write on the meaning and application to our lives. That this book is insightful should not surprise us; Jesus is profound. It is also practical, as following Jesus has to happen in real life now. As we read, we, too, will progress, perhaps fall back, get up, and try again as we follow Jesus. Jesus' love and presence will become more real, and His desire for us to be all that we can will motivate us.

Peter Roennfeldt has experienced what he writes about. Peter has been a pastor, evangelist, leader, church planter, trainer, motivator, mentor, public presenter, coach. Above everything else, though, he is a follower of Jesus. He has modeled the discipleship process with family, friends, and colleagues.

Peter has worked in Australia, the Pacific, Europe, Africa, and the

Middle East. He has traveled widely and shared his insights in most other parts of the world. He knows that the principles of following Jesus are applicable to illiterate subsistence farmers in the highlands of Papua New Guinea, sophisticated secular post-Christian professionals in the cities of northern and western Europe, nomadic Arab tribesmen in North Africa, and highly educated national and community leaders on educational campuses and across the communities of Africa, the Middle East, and Asia because he has ministered to these groups and many others.

Peter's passion is for believers in Jesus to become fully mature followers who disciple others. This book will encourage us to follow the methods of Jesus as much as holding to the beliefs of Jesus. As we follow Jesus together, He will build a disciple-making movement across generations and people groups.

I have personally been blessed as I have been mentored by Peter in the past. More recently, we have talked and prayed together as we have trained others in the principles of following Jesus. I am still learning to follow Jesus more closely, and this book will help me be more of who I want to be—and who He calls me to be.

Glenn Townend
pastor, church planter, denominational leader

EXPERIENCING
HIS WORLD

MANY GIVE JESUS little thought today, but two thousand years ago, He caught the attention of the masses, annoyed religious leaders, and confronted politicians. When about thirty, He stepped onto the stage from a small hilltop village of between 120 and 150 inhabitants,[1] bursting "the boundaries of all expectations"[2] and launching a countercultural movement that, within only three centuries, captivated millions across the Roman Empire.[3] His commitment to upside-down values, status reversal, and revolutionary teaching was breathtaking.

Jesus followed a simple process of disciplemaking, radically different from the religious and political leaders of His time. He connected with people (often around food), met their needs, and equipped them as disciples—to do what He was doing.

Disciples are protégés, learners or apprentices who multiply disciples by following Jesus' methods. They cultivate His movement, preparing people for His coming! The evening before His betrayal, He declared to His disciples: "Whoever believes in me will do the works I have been doing" (John 14:12). And, following His resurrection, He said, "As the Father has sent me, I am sending you" (John 20:21, compare John 17:18; Matthew 28:19).

To understand these words, we need to understand His world—the politics, the territorial jurisdictions, the threats of jealous despotic rulers, together with the topography, geography, culture, and religious practices of the society in which He lived. Where were the villages, towns, and cities situated? How did people live? What were their homes like? How were they furnished? What clothes were worn? What food was eaten? How did families function? Who was related? What were their fears and concerns?

In this book, we will discover Jesus' world. This reflects my own research from regular visits to Israel since 1979, including a season at the Jerusalem Study Centre with Dr. William Shea, only a block away from the Garden Tomb. But, more importantly, this book draws on the outstanding scholarship of Kenneth Bailey, Richard Horsley, Neil Asher Silberman, Craig Evans, Bargil Pixner, Peter Walker, and others.

From sitting beside Jacob's Well, sailing on Galilee, walking the Wadi Qelt, climbing the Mount of Olives and the Tower of Ascension, and visiting the Temple Mount, my realization grew that Jesus was not only the *message*, He was also the *method* for mission. I was confronted by His humanness. Favorite stories were radically revised, the mold into which Jesus had been shaped was broken, and my view of Him was challenged. The result: His life became my frame for evangelism and church planting, for my disciplemaking and movement thinking.

MY BASIC PREMISE

Jesus is our example in disciplemaking and movement building. It was not by chance that His movement went viral, so we will track His life as it unfolded, in sequence, to experience how He shaped disciples and cultivated a dynamic movement. All that is recorded by the Gospel writers contributes to our understanding, with five phases in His journey providing our frame:[4]

- *Phase One*: Preparation for a life of multiplication
- *Phase Two*: Foundations—modeling multiplication
- *Phase Three*: Participation—equipping for expanded outreach
- *Phase Four*: Leadership multiplication—movement through sacrificial love
- *Phase Five*: Movements—through Holy Spirit anointing

On this journey, we should also expect to rediscover what church could be—simple, in the relational streams of life. Jesus questioned the motivation for much religious activity, so expect to be unsettled by His attitude toward religion, but expect to resonate with the foundations, purpose, and essence of church as He established it.

Above all, expect to be inspired and encouraged. The Gospels provide the frame for a refreshing look into the life and ministry of Jesus Christ. Although fully God, His humanity is fully evident. His commitment to building His Kingdom movement is inspiring and informative.

A GOSPEL HARMONY

For this journey, along with your favorite Bible, I recommend using a "gospel harmony" such as R. L. Thomas and S. N. Gundry's *The NIV Harmony of the Gospels* or Steven L. Cox and Kendell H. Easley's *Harmony of the Gospels*.[5] A harmony provides sequence to the events of Jesus' life and ministry, bringing together the four Gospel stories the Bible offers us. Various harmonies reflect differences in the order of events, and some are referred to in this guide, but it is not our purpose to be definitive. Along with these guides you might read a life of Jesus, such as Jerry Thomas's *Messiah: A Contemporary Adaptation of a Classic on Jesus' Life, The Desire of Ages*.[6] If you prefer the original, *The Desire of Ages* has the same chapter numbering, so you can easily adapt your reading to those chapters.

A RIGOROUS BUT ENJOYABLE JOURNEY

This is a rigorous transformational trek, rather than a casual stroll. It takes you through the whole account of Jesus' life. This can be done as a lone hike or a journey shared with others. You might take sections at a time, using these guides to research specific aspects of Jesus' life and ministry. If you are working through this in a small group, you might want to commit to one section, perhaps take a break, then return for the next section. Or you might choose a section that is most relevant to your current experience or leadership roles. For example, Phase 4 might be used as a resource to explore the worldview and leadership principles Jesus used with His twelve apostles, or Phase 5 as a guided tour of Jesus' *passion week*, from Palm Sunday to Resurrection Sunday. But, for the whole journey, these guides are written for:

1. *Bible-reading and discussion groups.* In such groups, each person reads the Gospel sections, working through a guide, then the group

meets weekly for breakfast, in a café, or in an evening home group to discuss the application of key ideas and principles. It is a long journey, but participants get together at a time that suits them, for about an hour, inviting others to join. It is a great way to introduce friends to Jesus.

2. *Pastors equipping movement leaders.* Many ministry leaders and pastors are already using *Following Jesus* with their ministry teams. It is a year-long journey. Team members read the Gospels, work through one guide each week, then take an hour at a weekly team meeting to discuss the implications for their lives, ministries, and church.

3. *Movement, mission agency, and denominational leaders.* For those with teams of ministry leaders and administrative personnel, *Following Jesus* provides a frame for a weekly worship and discussion time. All are encouraged to read the Gospels, reflect on one guide each week, then participate in the group discussion. Or ministry coordinators and pastors in networks or denominations could use the guides in daily devotions, then be invited to a number of retreats over a year to integrate insights into their movements.

JOURNAL YOUR JOURNEY

This book invites, encourages, and even expects you to express your own responses, thoughts, and feelings. The questions are not rhetorical; the notes are not prescriptive of an expected answer. Rather, you are encouraged to clarify your own journey with Jesus.

For those who are minimal writers, we have included a small amount of space after each question and at the end of each guide to record responses in just a few words. But for the full and deeper experience with this book, we recommend that you take up the habit of journaling as you work through the life and ministry of Jesus.

To do this, get a notebook—it might be a good-quality journal or a cheap notepad. Or you might open a new document on your computer or tablet. Settle on a system of identifying your notes with the guide numbers used throughout the book, and record what you discover, see, experience, and care about.

As you read, give time to each question and record what is important to you. The questions are a prompt to reflect. And, of course, write down the questions that come to mind as you are working through these guides. Some of these might be answered as you progress further; others might be valuable to raise with friends you are sharing this journey with; and still others might be questions that you will continue to wrestle with.

Writing will convert the jumble of extraneous ideas or thoughts floating in your mind into coherent insights, values, and action plans. Jesus calls us to dig deep, but also to act—*to make disciples who make other disciples!* Writing clarifies which ideas are most important to you. So don't skim. Make this a year deep in the life and ministry of Jesus.

SHARE THE JOURNEY

For the past fifteen years, I have been part of a small group of men who meet for a café breakfast each Thursday at 6:45 a.m. to share God's Word, encourage each other, and pray together. Some of us travel a lot and some have moved inter-state and internationally, but the weekly group continues, both in person and online. The guides in this book could provide a frame for such a group—individual reading, reflection, comments shared on social media, with regular opportunities to discuss key discoveries. Who could you invite on this journey? And who among your friends or in your community would you like to see grow as followers of Jesus? Plan to share this journey with them. Be part of Jesus' movement of disciples making disciples!

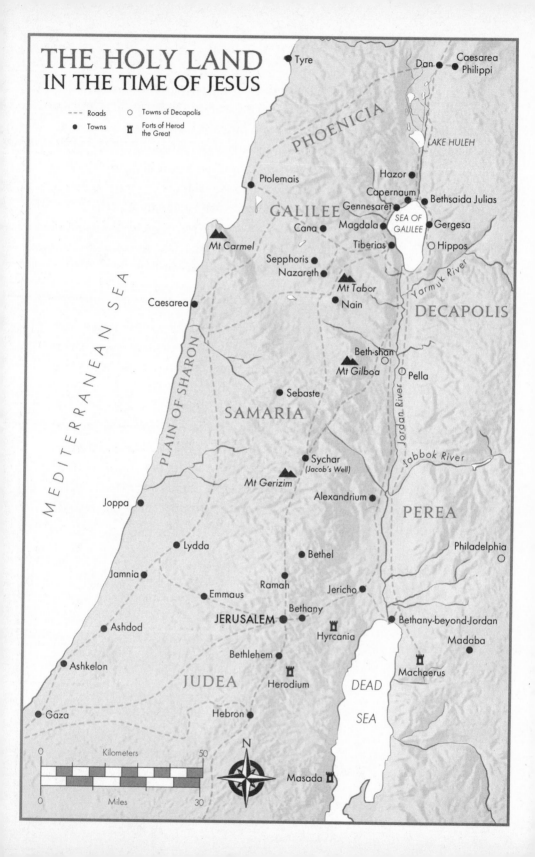

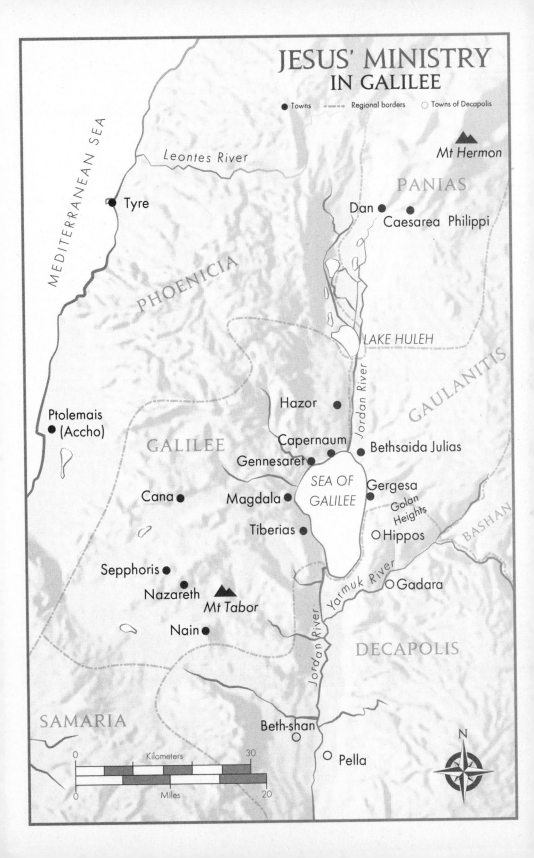

Preparation

FOR A LIFE OF MULTIPLICATION

THE FIRST THIRTY YEARS of Jesus' life were spent in preparation. Then, John the Baptist introduced Him and His short public ministry of disciplemaking. By the end of His ministry, Jesus commissioned His disciples to do the same: "Go and make disciples of all *nations*" (Matthew 28:19, emphasis added). Using the word *ethne*, Jesus indicated He was not speaking of nation states, but of making disciples in all people groups or *relational streams*.

The primary witnesses to Jesus' disciplemaking and movement building are the four Gospel writers:

- Matthew, a first-century tax collector who became a disciple, focuses on Jesus' radical, countercultural kingship and Kingdom and is the only one who mentions Jesus using the word *church*. Church formation is a byproduct of disciplemaking.

- John Mark, perhaps the cousin of Barnabas (Colossians 4:10),[1] recounts his story as perhaps heard from Peter the fisherman.[2]

- Luke, a Gentile doctor (Colossians 4:14) whose two contributions make up nearly 27 percent of the New Testament, wrote his "orderly account" after careful research (Luke 1:3), as he had not personally observed Jesus' life.

- Without John's Gospel, we would have little insight into Jesus' first eighteen months of ministry. Writing more than sixty years after Jesus' resurrection, John is the only Gospel writer who experienced the whole of Jesus' ministry. His Gospel is mostly chronological, highlighting crises and turning points, but his account does not begin with Bethlehem—or Jordan. Rather, Jesus is introduced as Creator and Savior, the Word of God and the Lamb of God "slain from the creation of the world" (John 1:1-3; Revelation 13:8). He then moves to John the Baptist's testimony about Jesus and Jesus inviting people to be disciples.

Matthew was the sermon reporter, Mark the biographer, Luke the historian, and John the theologian. We are also enriched by reading the letters of Paul, who wrote, "Your attitude should be the same as that of Christ Jesus: Who, being in very nature God, did not consider equality with God something to be grasped, but made himself nothing, taking the very nature of a servant [the original word is *slave*], being made in human likeness. And being found in appearance as a man, he humbled himself and became obedient to death—even death on a cross" (Philippians 2:5-8). He was made like us (Hebrews 2:5-18).

In this first phase, we reflect on Jesus' early years: His preparation for movement building. The guides cover sections 1–19 in *The NIV Harmony of the Gospels* and chapters 1–10 in *Messiah*. They begin with the prologues to Luke and John's Gospels, and Jesus' human ancestry, and end with His cousin John's ministry.

We explore questions such as: What did God experience and learn in becoming truly human? What can we learn from these preparation years? And what are the implications for us?

JESUS AS A BABY

LUKE'S GOSPEL PROLOGUE introduces his research into the life of Jesus, revealing his core convictions about Jesus and His Kingdom movement. Luke wrote of "all that Jesus *began* to do and to teach until the day he was taken up to heaven" (Acts 1:1-2).

READ
  - Luke 1:1–2:38; John 1:1-18; Matthew 1:1-25, compare Luke 3:23-38
  - *Messiah*, chapters 1–5

From where might Luke have gathered his information?[1]

_____

_____

In becoming a baby, what were some things God experienced for the first time?

_____

_____

Being fully God and fully human, Jesus chose to veil His divinity in humanity, living and ministering as a human. What did He give up to be human?

_____

_____

Why did Jesus do this?

_____

_____

What can we learn from Jesus' two family trees (Matthew 1:1-17; Luke 3:23-38)?

_____

_____

Who were the women in His ancestry (Matthew 1:3, 5, 6, 16)?

_____

_____

What kind of people were "His people," whom He came to save (Matthew 1:1-21)?

_____

_____

As soon as Mary learned she was pregnant, she went to see Elizabeth. What do Mary and Zechariah's songs reveal about Jesus' future ministry (Luke 1:46-55, 67-79)?

_____

_____

How much older was John the Baptist than Jesus?

_____

_____

How long did Mary stay with Elizabeth? So what would the village people in Nazareth have observed when she returned?

_____

_____

Learning of Mary's pregnancy, Joseph "considered this" (Matthew 1:20). The Greek word can also be translated that "he became angry."[2] *But, in the face of a community demanding her death for shaming the honor of her family and village, what strength of character did Joseph show in taking Mary as his wife?*

_____

_____

According to Luke's account, who were the first to welcome Jesus (Luke 2:1-20)?

_____

_____

FULLY GOD—FULLY HUMAN!

What important insights concerning Jesus do you find in these additional Scriptures (Philippians 2:1-11; Hebrews 2:14-18, 4:14-16, 5:7-10, and 10:19-25)?

_____

_____

God Almighty took on human form and entered our world. He chose to begin as a baby, not as a grown man. The Bible says that He "*made himself nothing*" (Philippians 2:7, emphasis added). He never ceased to be fully God, but He veiled His deity and intentionally limited Himself and His powers to become fully human. He was made like us "in every way" (Hebrews 2:17).

Jesus leaves heaven's glory for earth's insignificance. What a sacrifice on God's part to become one of us! The Creator enters creation, so that He might not only be our God, but also our high priest (Hebrews 2:17) and our way to God (John 14:6). What a strange and unusual way to save the world. God's gift to us was a baby.[3]

What were God's gifts to Him?[4]

- obedient parents (Luke 1:38 and Matthew 1:18-25);
- the names Immanuel and Jesus (Matthew 1:18-23); and
- birth announcements (Luke 2:8-40).

CULTURAL BACKGROUND

Have you noticed there is no reference in the Gospels to Jesus' birth in a stable? Nor does it say Jesus was born the night Mary and Joseph arrived in Bethlehem. Rather, Luke records Joseph and Mary went to Bethlehem to register, Mary was expecting, and "while they were there, the time came for the baby to be born" (Luke 2:6).

There is no suggestion of a breathless arrival in the village, with baby Jesus born that night! And it would have been unthinkable for Mary to be left without care, to give birth alone or with a man—Joseph—present. It is true: Bethlehem was crowded, but no Middle Eastern family would neglect a pregnant wife, and there is no suggestion this was the case. Just the opposite! The family guest rooms (called an "inn" but not meaning a commercial inn) were occupied.[5]

So what does the story suggest?

Imagine the excitement: "The time came for the baby to be born" (Luke 2:6). The women cleared the family living area where the cooking and baking was done, where the family slept each night. This space was adjacent to a lower area—maybe even a cave, from which the home extended[6]—where domestic animals stood and rested during the night, with their feeding troughs or "mangers" in the floor of the living space. The presence of the animals provided warmth for the family during the winter months. The men would have been banished, then the baby was born, wrapped and placed in the perfect crib, a "manger" in the heart of the home.

Meanwhile, the shepherds—rough and poor men—received the good news: Christ the Lord had been born, "wrapped . . . and lying in a manger" (Luke 2:12). Their being out in the fields at that time rules out the winter months (December to February) as the season of Jesus' birth. Although poor, these men understood the value of life—and babies. They went, found the baby as they had been told, and spread the word—"glorifying and praising God" (Luke 2:20). Jesus was born in poverty and welcomed by the poorest.[7]

REFLECTION

What was new for you in this section?

_____

_____

Why choose to follow God, who came into this world like us, as a baby?

_____

_____

SHARING

What will you share with friends on this journey with you?

_____

_____

What will you share with friends who don't follow Jesus?

_____

_____

JESUS AS A JEWISH CHILD

AS A JEWISH BABY, Jesus was circumcised at eight days old. A short time later, Mary and Joseph took the two-hour walk to the Jerusalem Temple to dedicate their baby to God. The city was then a major building site, with thousands of laborers working for Herod the Great to enlarge the temple. By the time the magi—or Gentile religious astrologers[1]— arrived to worship Jesus, He was a "child"—a Jewish child.

READ
- Matthew 2:1-23; Luke 2:39-52
- *Messiah*, chapters 6–8

According to Matthew's account, who were the first to welcome Him (Matthew 2:1-12)?

_____

_____

With the East dominated by animism, multiple gods, and idols, in what way would their arrival have been a surprise? Being from the East, what might have been their religious backgrounds?

_____

_____

What does this story suggest about Jesus' age at this time (Matthew 2:13-18)?

_____

_____

In what practical ways might the magi's gifts have been God the Father's provision for His Son?

_____

_____

An angel warned Joseph of the threat from Herod, and the family fled to Egypt. This was a formative stage in the little boy's life. While there was a strong Jewish colony in Egypt at the time, He would have played with Egyptian children, experiencing different food, languages, education systems, and culture. Perhaps He ran in the shadows of the pyramids—already more than two thousand years old—and swam in the Nile.

How might this land of Jewish captivity, at the time of Moses, have affected Jesus?

_____

_____

With news of Herod's death, the family returned to Israel. But, having been warned by an angel to avoid the territory of Herod Archelaus, they settled in Nazareth. There Jesus' education continued, taught by Mary, Joseph, and the rabbi in the local synagogue. As for other Jewish families, there was the annual Passover pilgrimage to Jerusalem. By the time He was twelve, perhaps celebrating His Bar Mitzvah—marking His development from a Jewish child to "a spiritually responsible person"—He had many questions (Luke 2:41-47).[2]

How might He have learned that Joseph was not His biological father?

_____

_____

When might Jesus have started connecting the dots between Bethlehem, Egypt, and Nazareth?

_____

_____

What might have been the impact of learning that little boys in Bethlehem had been killed as a result of His birth—and that He had escaped the slaughter?

MESSIANIC PROPHECIES

Three messianic prophecies—Old Testament Scriptures that identified Jesus as the promised Christ or Messiah—are mentioned in Matthew's story of Jesus' childhood:

1. the place of His birth (Micah 5:2);
2. the grief experienced by mothers, when their boys were killed (Jeremiah 31:15); and
3. the time He spent in Egypt (Hosea 11:1).

Jesus' return from Egypt, to grow up in Nazareth, was also seen as a fulfillment of the prophecy: "He would be called a Nazarene" (Matthew 2:23). Jerome, who translated the Bible (and died) in Bethlehem, traced Jesus' identification as a Nazarene to his being a "shoot" (*netzer*) of David (Isaiah 11:1-5) and therefore a member of the Natzorean or Davidide clan.[3]

HEROD THE GREAT

A number of Herods are mentioned in the New Testament. The one who sought to have Jesus murdered as a baby is known as Herod the Great (an Edomite), who ruled over Palestine by permission of the Roman Emperor from 37 BC. Distrustful and fearing for his throne, he wiped out all Hasmonean royalty in his own family, including the high priest, his brother-in-law, his favorite wife (Mariamne), two of his sons by her, as well as her mother (Alexandra). Nevertheless, he gained renown as the builder of magnificent structures including a winter palace at Jericho, the fortress of Masada, extensions to the Temple Mount, and the beautification of the Second Jewish Temple.

When news of the birth of a Davidian prince reached Herod, "he was disturbed, and all Jerusalem with him" (Matthew 2:3). Joseph was warned, and he immediately fled with Mary and the child Jesus to Egypt. Southeast from Jerusalem, in full view of Bethlehem and clearly visible from the Mount of Olives, was the Herodium: an artificial, cone-like mountain Herod constructed as a palace and mausoleum. When he died in 4 BC, his body was brought to the Herodium from Jericho and he was buried in a stone sarcophagus now on display in the Israel Museum.[4]

The territory of Herod the Great was then divided between three sons, each also known as "Herod": Archelaus (Idumea, Judea, and Samaria); Antipas (Galilee and Perea); and Philip (Trachonitis). On learning Herod the Great had died, the family of Jesus returned from Egypt, but Joseph was again warned away from Judea, where Herod's violent son Archelaus ruled.

NAZARETH

Joseph took the family to Nazareth, in the lower hills of Galilee. Some suggest this village had been settled 100 years earlier by descendants of Israel's King David as a Jewish colony in Gentile territory, as a deliberate plan to keep their "royal" line pure and to re-Judaize Galilee. But research indicates most of the towns and villages of Galilee were Jewish. In Nazareth, there was a synagogue and *mikvah* (a pool used for ritual immersion in Judaism)[5] but no pagan temples or schools. Craig Evans observes, "In all likelihood not a single non-Jew lived in Nazareth at the time."[6] There, Jesus grew up, in a village of about twenty houses with as few as 120 to 150 inhabitants.[7]

REFLECTION

As you read through the notes and Bible references in this guide, what stood out to you?

What does it mean for you to know that Jesus grew up as a Jewish boy?

SHARING

What will you contribute to the discussion with your friends sharing this journey?

_____

_____

What will you share with friends who don't now follow Jesus?

_____

_____

JESUS THE CARPENTER

DURING HIS TEEN and young-adult years, Jesus lived in Nazareth, where He was known as both "the carpenter's son" and "the carpenter." He had brothers—James, Joseph, Simon, and Judas—and sisters whose names are not recorded in the Gospels (Matthew 13:55, 56; Mark 6:3).

READ
- Luke 3:1-3, 21-23 (first part); Matthew 13:53-58; Mark 6:1-6
- *Messiah*, chapter 9

Consider Jesus' humanity. In what ways did Jesus grow and develop? And what temptations might He have faced as a teen (Hebrews 2:17, 18, 4:15)?

_____

_____

Read Isaiah 52:13–53:12 and reflect on what these prophecies foretell about Jesus' young-adult years:

What do we know about His physical appearance?

_____

_____

How would peers have related to a teenage boy with no likeness to His father?

_____

_____

How might Jesus have suffered as a teen and young man?

_____

_____

Read Psalm 69:6-12. (Compare Psalm 69:9 with John 2:17, which suggests Psalm 69 is about Jesus, and maybe His teen and young-adult years.)

Why might His own brothers have scorned Him as a stranger—and the community made Him the butt of their jokes and mockery (Psalm 69:7-12)?

_____

_____

WORKING-CLASS JESUS

Jesus was a "blue-collar" worker or manual laborer. How might village life and the family business have prepared Him for ministry?

_____

_____

Imagine the family home. Is there any evidence He was the youngest or oldest? How might Jesus have related to His brothers and sisters—and to other young men and women?

_____

_____

NAZARETH AND SEPPHORIS

Although small, Nazareth was not isolated. Just south was a vantage point from which Jesus could see the Plain of Jezreel, through which passed the Via Maris, the Roman road carrying traffic from Syria through Galilee to the Mediterranean and Egypt. About four miles to the northwest, within easy walking distance, was Sepphoris, capital of Galilee. The Romans had razed this city in response to a Jewish revolt following the death of Herod the Great, but Herod Antipas had the city rebuilt. As a major building site during Jesus' teen and young-adult years, it provided ready employment for a *tekton*—a worker "in stone as well as in wood"[1]—such as Joseph and Jesus.

Archaeological evidence indicates that, in Jesus' time (pre–AD 70), Sepphoris was "thoroughly Jewish," with many *mikva'ot* (immersion pools), lamp fragments depicting the menorah (seven-branched candlestick), more than one hundred fragments of stone vessels—preferred by Jews as they could not be made "unclean"—as well as no coins depicting Roman emperors or pagan deities, no pagan buildings or idols, and no pig bones in the city dump. After AD 70, this changed dramatically.[2]

There might also have been employment on the shores of Galilee when Antipas moved his capital to Tiberias in AD 20, but Sepphoris remained an important center. Although there is no specific reference to Jesus visiting these towns, He was certainly familiar with urban life.[3] It might have been in these cities that Jesus first learned about:

- planning well before building a tower (Luke 14:28-30);
- laying foundations on rock, not sand (Matthew 7:24-27); and
- the term *hypocrite*, describing actors' use of masks to perform the roles of many characters in Greek plays (Matthew 23:13).[4]

REFLECTION

As you reflect on this guide, what struck you as new or important?

_____

_____

How does knowing Jesus was a teenager in Nazareth—working as a builder's laborer and carpenter, perhaps in Sepphoris—influence your decision to follow Him?

_____

_____

SHARING

What will you share with your friends who are already on this journey?

_____

_____

What will you share with those you would like to see on this journey with Jesus?

_____

_____

JESUS' COUSIN

Preparing the Way for the Kingdom

JOHN THE BAPTIST was chosen by God to prepare the way for Jesus and His Kingdom movement. His role had been foretold.

READ

- Matthew 3:1-12; Mark 1:1-8; Luke 1:5-25, 67-80, 3:1-20; John 1:19-28
- *Messiah*, chapter 10

Compare Matthew 3:1-3 (see also Mark 1:1-3; Luke 3:1-6) with Isaiah 40:1-3. What are your observations?

_____

_____

According to the prophecy of his father Zechariah, speaking when filled with the Holy Spirit, what was John's role to be (Luke 1:67-80)?

_____

_____

John the Baptist played a key part in preparing the people for Jesus and His Kingdom. A typical prophet, he was an eccentric in many ways. He looked like a prophet, dressed like a prophet, and sounded like a prophet. Where and how did John live (Luke 1:80; Matthew 3:4; Mark 1:6)?

_____

_____

The Jewish people were waiting for God to send the long-promised Messiah to save them from their Roman oppressors. When John began preaching, they were ready. They poured out of the cities and towns of the region to hear him. Try to imagine the scenes described (Matthew 3:5-10; Mark 1:5; Luke 3:7-15). Who was being baptized—and where?

_____

_____

Except in flood, the Jordan River is small (30 to 50 feet across), but it was associated with making a new start. The Israelites crossed it to enter their Promised Land. Here Joshua took over from Moses, and Elisha from Elijah. It became the eastern border of their land. And from this muddy stream, Naaman the Syrian rose clean of leprosy, confessing, "Now I know that there is no God in all the world except in Israel" (2 Kings 5:15). It is no coincidence this was the place for John's ministry. He was offering a new start to Israel—and for all.[1]

What could they no longer rely on? (This was a radical message for them: Luke 3:8.)

_____

_____

Why do you think the people wanted to be right with God, confessing their sins and identifying with this prophet-preacher through baptism?

_____

_____

For whom were they waiting?

_____

_____

What was John's message (Mark 1:7-8; Matthew 3:11-12; Luke 3:16-18)?

_____

_____

John was a member of Jesus' extended family (Luke 1:36), a close friend (John 3:22-30), and the first to understand Jesus' mission as the Lamb of God (John 1:29-35). He was the one chosen to prepare the way for Jesus and His Kingdom.

THE EXPECTATIONS

It was a desperate time for the Jewish people. Suffering under severe Roman oppression, they longed for the deliverance promised by their prophets. The last Old Testament prophet, Malachi, had foretold the return of Elijah the prophet (Malachi 4:5-6), and here was John the Baptist on the other side of the Jordan, preaching in the same wilderness from which Elijah had ascended.

Consider what the angel Gabriel said when he broke the four-hundred-year silence of the inter-Testament period:

- Luke 1:13-17: John would go "before the Lord, in the spirit and power of Elijah."
- Matthew 11:14, compare Matthew 17:1-13: Jesus said John "is the Elijah who was to come."

It was also the timing. Luke indicates that John began baptizing in "the fifteenth year of the reign of Tiberius Caesar—when Pontius Pilate was governor of Judea, Herod tetrarch of Galilee, his brother Philip tetrarch of Iturea and Traconitis, and Lysanias tetrarch of Abilene—during the high priesthood of Annas and Caiaphas" (Luke 3:1-2). That was AD 27, when Jesus "was about thirty years old" (Luke 3:23).

In response to his prayer for the salvation of his people and city (Daniel 9:4-19), Daniel the prophet had been told that from "the issuing of the decree to restore and rebuild Jerusalem" (457 BC) it would be "seven 'sevens,' and sixty-two 'sevens'" (483 years), until "the Anointed One, the ruler, comes" (Daniel 9:25). Jesus was baptized and anointed right on time. Paul wrote: "When the time had fully come, God sent his Son, born of a woman, born under law, to redeem those under law, that we might receive the full rights of [children]" (Galatians 4:4-5).

The timing was right. John the Baptist fitted their expectations for the return of Elijah and, they wondered, could he be the Messiah?

THE *PERSON OF PEACE*—KEY TO MOVEMENT BUILDING

John the Baptist was chosen by God to prepare the way for Jesus, to intentionally connect Him with the people! Jesus called such key people *persons of peace* (Luke 10:5-6). Those with relationships into other streams beyond their rank, background, or ethnicity could be called *bridges of God*,[2] linking to *persons of peace* in those streams.

ESSENTIAL FRAMES OF JESUS' MOVEMENT BUILDING

- *The person:* Jesus. This is the Kingdom movement of Jesus the King, and through Him, the incarnation of God, both the gospel of the Kingdom (the *message*) and the process of movement building (the *method*) are revealed.

- *The principle:* Status reversal. Fully God, He became fully human—a baby, child, young man, "a blue-collar messiah."[3] This is ultimate subordination, the very nature of the triune God. Transformation comes from below: "The Path of Descent is the theme of themes, the meta-narrative"—master story—of the Bible.[4]

- *The purpose:* To do the Father's will. This was Jesus' mission—and ours.

- *The person of peace:* Key in relational streams. Because of their reputation—good or bad—such people have influence when they become followers of Jesus and are key to making disciples in the social or relational streams of society where decisions are made.

Can you suggest other key ingredients of Jesus' movement building?

REFLECTION

What has impressed you with John's story?

_____

_____

In choosing to follow Jesus, what is important to you about His first thirty years of life?

_____

_____

SHARING

What will you share with your friends who are on this journey with you?

_____

_____

What has this preparation phase of Jesus' life come to mean for you?

_____

_____

How has God been shaping your life—and for what purpose?

_____

_____

From this preparation phase of Jesus' life, what will you share with those you are encouraging to know Jesus better?

_____

_____

Foundations

MODELING MULTIPLICATION

THE SECOND PHASE of Jesus' ministry lasted about eighteen months, from His baptism to His move to Galilee. It is often referred to as His early Judean ministry. While each Gospel writer tells of the transition experiences from *preparation* to this *ministry foundation* phase, John alone tells the stories of this time—and what significant accounts they are!—including the stories of:

- Jesus calling His first disciples, introducing five invitations of disciplemaking;
- Jesus' total reliance on Holy Spirit POWER[1]; and
- Jesus redefining the meaning of the Second Temple, introducing Himself as the new temple!

His actions on the Temple Mount during His first visit to Jerusalem were foundational to His Kingdom movement. This was no mere "cleansing" of the Temple. He was declaring himself to be the temple—the One in whom God was present!

This foundation phase is marked by radical illustrations of the nature and scope of His Kingdom and temple ministry:

- an interview with a Jewish Council member, Nicodemus;
- explosive growth in the number of His disciples in the Judean countryside;
- a visit with a Samaritan woman, with a whole village becoming believers; and
- healing a royal official's son in Capernaum—from Cana.

We are in for an interesting journey of discovery as we explore sections 20–36 in *The NIV Harmony of the Gospels*—and, if you are also reading *Messiah*, chapters 11–20. These sections include the transitional events into this second phase of Jesus' ministry: His baptism by John the Baptist and being led by the Spirit into the wilderness. Identified as "the Lamb of God" and "Son of God," Jesus calls His first disciples and lays down the foundations of His movement. This phase reaches through to John's imprisonment, signaling transition to Jesus' third phase of movement building (Luke 3:20; Mark 1:14).

TRANSITION EXPERIENCES

Jesus' Baptism and Temptations

JESUS WAS ABOUT thirty years old when He began ministry (Luke 3:23). His transition from village life to public life involved two critical experiences—His baptism and temptations—and two announcements. Because we have become familiar with these stories, they might not seem unusual, but His baptism was "with water for repentance" (Matthew 3:11), even though He was "the holy one" without sin (Luke 1:35). And He was "led by the Spirit into the desert to be tempted by the devil" (see Matthew 4:1); yet, surely the Spirit is to protect from evil. Through His baptism and temptations, Jesus further identified with those He had come to save, demonstrating God's nature.

READ

- Matthew 3:1–4:12; Mark 1:9-13; Luke 3:1-3, 21-23, 4:1-13; John 1:15-35
- *Messiah*, chapters 11–13

JESUS' BAPTISM

John the Baptist lived in desert isolation, eating locusts and wild honey. His message was a scathing rebuke of sin, a call to "produce fruit in keeping with repentance." Those who confessed were baptized in the muddy Jordan River (Matthew 3:6, 8).

What comparison did John draw, and what did he predict of Jesus (Matthew 3:11-12, compare Mark 1:7-8; Luke 3:15-18; John 1:32-34)?

_____

_____

Why would Jesus participate in a baptism of repentance, despite John's protest (Matthew 3:13–15)?

_____

_____

This is the first time Matthew records Jesus using the word righteousness. It became a key word in Jesus' vocabulary and in Matthew's Gospel. What did Jesus mean by saying, "It is proper for us to do this to fulfill all righteousness" (Matthew 3:15)?

_____

_____

Jesus was not baptized as an example, but "to fulfill all righteousness."[1] Jesus is "God with us." Was He seeking to reveal the very nature and attitude of God's heart? Was Jesus saying to John: "God is like me! He loves this milling crowd in the heat and dust on Jordan's banks. To see the nature of God, you must see Him standing in this water, dripping with mud and reeds, shoulder to shoulder with the most desperate of sinners!" Try to picture the scene. How does it impact you?

_____

_____

ANNOUNCEMENT FROM HEAVEN

Immediately after His baptism, Jesus paused to pray. What was the Holy Spirit's response (Luke 3:21-23, compare Matthew 3:16-17; Mark 1:9-11)?

_____

_____

What was the significance of the Holy Spirit's action (Acts 10:34-38)?

_____

_____

What name or title was given to Jesus to signify this anointing?

_____

_____

What did the Father reveal about Jesus?

_____

_____

How do you think Jesus felt hearing His Father's voice (after thirty years)?

_____

_____

JESUS' TEMPTATIONS

"Then Jesus was *led by the Spirit* into the desert to be tempted *by the devil*" (Matthew 4:1, emphasis added; compare Mark 1:12-13; Luke 4:1-13). Jesus was tempted on different levels (Matthew 4:2-10). He met each temptation with God's Word:

- *Appetite:* "It is written _____" (Matthew 4:4).
- *Trust:* "It is written _____" (Matthew 4:7).
- *Control:* "It is written _____" (Matthew 4:10).

Why were the devil's shortcuts appealing? What were the implications for Jesus and us?

- To satisfy His hunger:

  _____

  _____

- To jump from the temple:

  _____

  _____

- To bow before the prince of this world:

  _____

  _____

Why do you think the Holy Spirit led Jesus to temptation?

_____

_____

Why do you think Luke lists the temptations in a different order from Matthew's Gospel?

_____

_____

What is the value of this wilderness experience? Was it—as with His baptism—to demonstrate God's nature, fully identifying with humanity and enduring the assaults of the evil one?

_____

_____

His baptism and temptations were revelations of the triune God. The Father, Son, and Spirit were One—living in "the neighborhood" (John 1:14, MSG) and working in perfect harmony. How do you respond to these experiences of Jesus?

_____

_____

ANNOUNCEMENT BY JOHN

After the temptations, "the devil left him, and angels came and attended him" (Matthew 4:11). Then Jesus returned to see His cousin at Bethany-beyond-Jordan.

What titles did John the Baptist give to Jesus?
 • John 1:29, 36:

_____

_____

 • John 1:34:

_____

_____

How did the Holy Spirit's anointing confirm John's convictions (John 1:32-34)?

_____

_____

From our perspective, these are radical experiences of status reversal—demeaning, even humiliating! But God's nature and ways are totally different from ours. Our political, corporate, and religious systems and hierarchies—maintaining power by coercion, competition, or collective self-interest—stand in stark contrast to God's total devotion to others and their interests. Jesus was King of a radically different kingdom!

A NEW BAPTISM

Through baptism, multitudes identified with John the Baptist—God's messenger—and his message of repentance. By His baptism, representing the triune God, as well as His message and mission, Jesus identified with those He had come to save. The Father affirmed Him, and the Holy Spirit anointed Him.

John prophesied a new baptism: "I baptize you with water for repentance. But after me will come one who is more powerful than I, whose sandals I am not fit to carry. *He will baptize you with the Holy Spirit and with fire*" (Matthew 3:11, emphasis added). Jesus came to bring baptism by the Holy Spirit—and to establish God's Kingdom movement.

What did Jesus say would be the evidence of Holy Spirit baptism (Acts 1:4-8)?

_____

_____

When you come to Jesus, you receive a new identity (Galatians 3:26-27; 2 Corinthians 5:17). Mark Edwards urges: "Allow your identity in Jesus to grow in you. Embrace your new identity as a child of God, deeply loved by Him and well pleasing to Him."[2]

What do these verses tell us about our identity in Christ?[3]

- 1 Corinthians 3:16: _____

_____

- 1 Corinthians 12:27: _____

_____

- 2 Corinthians 5:17: _____

_____

- Galatians 3:26-27: _____

_____

- Galatians 4:4-7: _____

_____

- Ephesians 2:10: _____
  _____

- Philippians 3:20: _____
  _____

- Philippians 4:13: _____
  _____

- Colossians 2:10: _____
  _____

- Colossians 3:3-4: _____
  _____

- 1 John 3:1-3 (don't miss this!): _____
  _____

REFLECTION

What was new for you in these transition experiences?

_____

_____

How are you declaring your identity with Jesus?

_____

_____

Imagine being isolated in a desert for forty days, without food or water and facing the constant barrage of the evil one. How might circumstances intensify these temptations?

_____

_____

SHARING

What will you share with friends on this journey with you?

_____

_____

What could you share with those you are encouraging to know Jesus better?

_____

_____

"COME AND SEE"

Jesus Calls His First Disciples

JESUS' BAPTISM and temptations marked the beginning of His public life in Judea. Matthew, Mark, and Luke did not write of this early Judean ministry. They moved from His temptations directly to John the Baptist's imprisonment and Jesus' relocation back to Galilee. John alone provides insights into Jesus' first eighteen months of ministry, which fits between Matthew 4:11-12, Mark 1:13-14, and Luke 4:13-14. Writing decades after the other Gospel writers, John included experiences they had not, to reveal Jesus' identity as "the Christ, the Son of God" (John 20:30-31).

The first thing Jesus did in public life was invite people to become disciples. He used five invitations—foundational to working with individuals, as well as to His movement building. To unbelievers, Jesus said, "Come and see"; while to believers, He said, "Follow me." What He did in this *ministry foundation* phase He continued to do even on the cross, evangelizing the unbeliever next to Him and edifying believers watching Him.[1] Jesus modeled disciplemaking, and we will find His approach practical and relevant today.

READ
- John 1:19-51
- *Messiah*, chapter 14

Why do you think Jesus looked for His first disciples among John's disciples?

_____

_____

How did John point His disciples to Jesus, and what did they do (John 1:35-37)?

_____

_____

INVITATION 1: "COME AND SEE"

The conversation between Jesus and these men was direct and simple (John 1:38-39).

What was Jesus' invitation?

_____

_____

In many cultures today, an invitation "for coffee" involves visiting for an hour or so—without necessarily even drinking coffee! In a similar way, Jesus was inviting John's disciples to spend time, to enjoy food and drink, to stay and talk. How long did they stay?

_____

_____

After spending time with Jesus, Andrew reported: "We have found the Messiah" (John 1:40-45).

What had John the Baptist said to pique their interest?

_____

_____

In the light of John 1:44-45, what might Jesus have shared as evidence?

_____

_____

PICTURES OF JESUS

Review the way Jesus was introduced by the Gospel writers:

Matthew focused on Jesus the King, His Kingdom, and the character of His subjects: "Jesus Christ the son of David, the son of Abraham" (Matthew 1:1). In Matthew's Gospel, He was called:

- Jesus, "because he will save his people from their sins" (Matthew 1:21).
- Immanuel, "which means 'God with us'" (Matthew 1:23).
- The "king of the Jews," before whom the magi "bowed down and worshiped" (Matthew 2:2, 11).

Mark introduced Him as "Jesus Christ, the Son of God" (Mark 1:1). Luke declared His name to be Jesus (Luke 1:31). He was called:

- The "Son of the Most High," whose "kingdom will never end" (Luke 1:32-33).
- The "holy one"—"the Son of God" (Luke 1:35).
- "Christ the Lord" (Luke 2:11) and "the Lord's Christ" (Luke 2:26).

John waited more than sixty years before writing. He no doubt read the accounts of Matthew, Mark, and Luke. With Jesus' entire life and ministry in mind, He selected the turning points and crises. His interest was the significance of each, rather than the event itself. Like Matthew, He reported Jesus' discussions in detail, but John focused on the nature of Jesus, the incarnate Son of God. He wrote: "In the beginning was the Word, and the Word was with God, and the Word was God. He was with God in the beginning" (John 1:1-2), and

- "Through him all things were made" (John 1:3).
- "In him was life, and that life was the light of men" (John 1:4).
- "The Word became flesh and made his dwelling among us" (John 1:14).

OVERVIEW OF FIVE INVITATIONS

Jesus extended five invitations to make disciples for His Kingdom. These undergirded His movement building and parallel the phases of His ministry:

1. "Come and see" was an invitation to experience who He was.
2. "Follow me" invited people into relationship with Him.
3. "Come fishing" drew them into participation.

4. "Love your enemies" challenged them to countercultural, sacrificial living.
5. "Receive the Spirit" was an invitation to receive empowerment for the authentic replication of His ministry.

These invitations provide a frame for our task of *making disciples who multiply other disciples!*

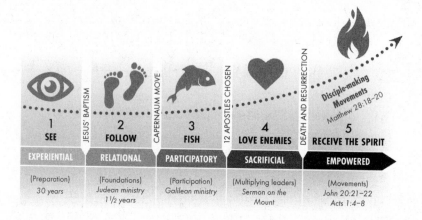

REFLECTION

What has stood out to you in this section?

_____

_____

What is your response to Jesus' first invitation?

_____

_____

SHARING

What will you share with your friends?

_____

_____

In what practical settings and ways might you extend the invitation to "Come and see" to people you would like to become disciples of Jesus?

_____

_____

"FOLLOW ME"

Jesus' Second Invitation

JESUS' STRATEGY for making disciples was simple. In the previous guide, we saw how He challenged people to "come and see." He spent time with them so they could experience what He was like and He could explain who He was. He used the Scriptures familiar to them: the writings of Moses, the Psalms, and the Prophets.

It is interesting to see how naturally His new disciples picked up on His *method*, multiplying what He was doing. Having spent just a day with Jesus, Andrew announced to Peter, "We have found the Messiah." And Philip said to Nathanael, "We have found the one Moses wrote about in the Law, and about whom the prophets also wrote," inviting him to "Come and see" (John 1:35-46).

Jesus' second invitation was "Follow me." This was an invitation to share a relational journey. Again, it took an investment of time. Disciplemaking is not limited to a seminar or Bible study; rather it is *living on the path of life* together.

READ
- John 1:35–2:12
- *Messiah*, chapter 15

INVITATION 2: "FOLLOW ME"

Jesus was going back to Galilee and wanted Philip to go with Him. What was His invitation (John 1:43)?

What was Nathanael's reaction to Philip's excitement (John 1:45-46)?

BACKGROUND

While Philip, Andrew, and Peter came from Bethsaida (John 1:44), a fishing town just east of the Jordan at the northern end of the Sea of Galilee, Nathanael was from the village of "Cana in Galilee" (John 21:2). There is dispute as to its location: Was it *Kafr Kanna* just to the north and over the hill from Nazareth or *Khirbet Kana* a little further (eight miles) to the northeast?[1]

Nathanael might not have known Jesus personally, but he may have been aware of the family. Philip said: "We have found the one Moses wrote about in the Law, and about whom the prophets also wrote— Jesus of Nazareth, the son of Joseph" (John 1:45). In Nathanael's response—"Nazareth! Can anything good come from there?" (John 1:46)—he was saying, "No way! You're kidding, from that village? We know the family!"

But, in saying, "Follow me," Jesus revealed the truth of who He was (John 2:1-12):

Jesus was truly human. He wanted disciples to know Him, His family, where He came from, and who He was.

Where did Jesus take His first disciples?

What does this indicate about His priorities?

Jesus took His small band of disciples to Cana, a short walk from where He grew up, to celebrate a family wedding. As in His home village, children cared for sheep, goats, and donkeys; they helped with grain harvest and threshing, gathered olives and grapes in season, and watched as men worked the heavy olive press and women trod the grapes. Village homes built of fieldstones and mud were centers of activity: wool being spun and dyed, garments made, fruit dried, meat smoked, and food preserved and stored for winter. Jesus brought His disciples home, to embrace His mother, shake hands with His brothers, and greet His sisters.[2]

Jesus was truly God. He had veiled His divinity within His humanity. He indicated the time to reveal His identity had not yet come (John 2:4)—but mothers will persist!

What do you think might have been Mary's expectations?

_____

_____

Jesus generously blessed the festivities with a liberal supply of wine. By this first miraculous sign, "He thus revealed his glory" (John 2:11). What might this mean?

_____

_____

By the end of the wedding celebrations, what had Jesus' disciples learned about Him?

_____

_____

Having met His family, the disciples went with Jesus, along "with his mother and brothers," to Capernaum, where "they stayed for a few days" (John 2:12). His disciplemaking was on the path of everyday life. Did those few days provide an opportunity for Jesus and His family to meet His disciples' families, to better understand them and their responsibilities? Was there time for a little fishing, or reflection and preparation for His Passover visit to Jerusalem (John 2:13)?

EXPECTATIONS

John the Baptist lived in the wilderness from which the Old Testament prophet Elijah had ascended. John looked and sounded like a prophet; in contrast, Jesus didn't look or sound like the messiah the Jews expected or had in mind. Almost 170 years earlier, Judas Maccabeus had shaped their messianic expectations.[3]

The conquests of Alexander the Great extended the borders of the Grecian Empire, and the process of hellenization saturated vassal states with Greek culture, robbing "them of their identity" and thereby making "them less rebellious." Michael Frost observes: "In Israel, the process of hellenization was a dazzling success. The Jewish religion was not stamped out or forbidden by the Greeks. It was gradually abandoned as old-fashioned and useless."[4] The Seleucid monarch, Antiochus IV, thought that because Judaism was so weakened, the time was right to wipe it out. He declared himself to be the Greek god Zeus and ordered Jews to sacrifice and eat swine's flesh.

At Modien, a small town fifteen miles from Jerusalem, the old priest Matthias refused. He killed a young Jew who stepped forward to comply, together with the government representative, and fled with his five sons to wage guerrilla warfare on their oppressors.

Old Matthias handed leadership of the rebellion to his third son, Judas, before dying the next year (166 BC). Judas won unexpected victories and, although slain in 160 BC, leaving his brothers to continue "the struggle until Israel's freedom was won in 143 BC," "he was their great liberator."[5]

In 63 BC, Israel again lost freedom, this time to the Roman Empire. By the time Jesus arrived, they were desperately awaiting the arrival of a courageous Judas Maccabeus-type to deliver them from their Roman oppressors and to restore their dignity. Jesus was not the fiery, passionate revolutionary they had in mind! They wanted a kingly messiah who would drive out the hated Romans.

REFLECTION

If Jesus did not match their messianic expectations, why did His disciples follow?

How have you decided to follow Jesus? What does that mean to you?

_____

_____

SHARING

What will you share with your friends who are on this journey with you?

_____

_____

What will you share with those you are encouraging to become disciples of Jesus?

_____

_____

JESUS' RELIANCE ON HOLY SPIRIT POWER

IN THIS GUIDE, we will review the experiences of Jesus as he transitioned from His years of *preparation* to this *ministry foundation* phase, to identify some of His priorities for life and disciplemaking. We will borrow the acronym POWER[1] to explore six priorities.

We will discover each in the experience of Jesus, reflect on what they meant to Him, and identify how to cultivate these priorities in our disciplemaking and our participation in God's Kingdom movement.

READ

- Matthew 3:1–4:12; Mark 1:9-13; Luke 3:1-3, 21-23, 4:1-13; John 1:15–2:12

HOLY SPIRIT POWER

1. Dependence. Jesus was conceived, anointed, and filled by the Holy Spirit.

How is Jesus' dependence on the Holy Spirit illustrated (Matthew 3:13–4:1)?

_____

_____

How will you cultivate Holy Spirit dependence in your life?

_____

_____

What steps will you take to ensure such dependence in disciplemaking?

_____

_____

2. *Prayer.* After His baptism, Jesus paused to pray.

Imagine Jesus' baptism and Him praying. What did He experience (Luke 3:21-22)?

_____

_____

How dependent are you on prayer? In what ways does prayer empower you?

_____

_____

What will you do to cultivate prayer in your ministry or movement?

_____

_____

3. *Obedience.* Jesus demonstrated obedience to God's Kingdom agenda.

What do you see as evidence of this priority for Jesus (Matthew 3:13–4:11)?

_____

_____

In what ways does your life reflect obedience to God's Kingdom agenda?

_____

_____

What changes are needed for your ministry or movement to reflect this priority?

_____

_____

4. *Word* of God.

How did Jesus relate to Scripture as the Word of God (Matthew 4:1-10; John 1:35-45)?

_____

_____

In what way is the Word a feature of your daily speech?

_____

_____

How might we engage with the Word of God in a way that transforms our lives?

_____

_____

Is the Word spreading or increasing (Acts 6:7) in your movement?

_____

_____

5. *Exalting* the Father:

What did Jesus do and say during His baptism and temptations that demonstrates this priority?

_____

_____

In what ways is it seen that you exalt the Father?

_____

_____

How does your life, vocation, and service exalt the Father?

_____

_____

6. *Relationships* intentionally cultivated:

Jesus was intentionally relational, as illustrated in John 1:35-39. What other examples can you think of in the Gospels?

_____

_____

With whom are you intentionally speaking about Jesus—to make disciples?

_____

_____

In what ways are those in your movement intentionally building relationships to make disciples?

_____

_____

Jesus lived by these Holy Spirit POWER priorities. They undergirded His life. What other priorities do you identify in Jesus' life?

_____

_____

REFLECTION

What fresh insight have you gained from Jesus' reliance upon Holy Spirit POWER?

_____

_____

What practical steps could you take to engage with Holy Spirit POWER?

_____

_____

SHARING

What is your response to the priorities of Jesus' life?

_____

_____

How will you share Jesus' priorities with those who are not yet His followers?

_____

_____

JESUS, THE ONE TEMPLE!

AFTER THE WEDDING at Cana and a few days beside Galilee, Jesus went "up" to Jerusalem for Passover (John 2:13). This Jewish feast originated at the time God delivered the Israelites from Egyptian captivity. Each year the Jewish people went to the Jerusalem Temple to celebrate. The Temple was the symbol of God's presence with His people. It was the place of healing, forgiveness, and worship. Jesus' actions on the Temple Mount during this visit were foundational to His Kingdom movement.

READ
- John 2:12-25
- *Messiah*, chapter 16

At the wedding feast in Cana, Jesus said to Mary, "My time has not yet come" (John 2:4). But, when He arrived "in the temple courts," what did He do (John 2:14-17)?

_____

_____

The Torah required cattle, sheep, and doves for their offerings (Leviticus 1:1-17), so what were the implications of Jesus driving them out?

_____

_____

What was Jesus' complaint against the money changers?

_____

_____

THE MONEY CHANGERS

Families traveled great distances for the Passover festivities and to offer sacrifices. Thousands of lambs, driven in from the Judean hills, were needed.[1] But the weary pilgrims were frustrated by the unfavorable exchange rates and exorbitant prices demanded by money changers for Tyrian shekels, the required temple coinage.[2]

These money changers were the temple gatekeepers, determining who went in and how far. A non-Jew could only get to the outer square, the *Court of the Gentiles*, where the money changers worked. A Jewish woman could go a little further, but only Jewish men (without physical disfigurement) could enter the *Court of Israel*. Beyond this, only the priests entered, with the chief priest alone allowed into the Holy of Holies on the Day of Atonement. How close one could get to the Most Holy Place reflected one's status in Jewish society.

Jesus surely knew He was asking for trouble by undermining the temple system as one of His first ministry acts. This was no mere cleansing of the temple. He was replacing the temple with Himself.

What do you think the disciples might have been thinking?

_____

_____

What did the Jews demand, and why (John 2:18)?

_____

_____

What was Jesus' confronting reply (John 2:19)?

_____

_____

How did the Jews understand this (John 2:20)?

_____

_____

The date of this Passover visit: The remark by His audience that it had "taken forty-six years to build this temple" helps us date this event. Herod the Great began this construction in 18 BC. Therefore, the year of this Passover was AD 28 (18 + 28 = 46).[3]

But what was Jesus speaking of (John 2:21-22)?

_____

_____

Having driven out the cattle, sheep, doves, and money changers, and claiming to be the true temple, Jesus performed "miraculous signs," healing and forgiving people in the city and in their homes. What was He demonstrating by these actions (John 2:23-25)?

_____

_____

A one-man temple system: Declaring war on its massive bureaucracy, Jesus set Himself up as a "rival" temple—"the Temple of God in person."[4] He healed and forgave wherever He went, making the Jerusalem Temple "redundant, irrelevant and obsolete." Steve Chalke describes Jesus' daily actions as "a massive threat to the entire religious, political and social fabric of Israel."[5]

DECONSTRUCTING THE TEMPLE SYSTEM

This Passover visit and declaration that He was the temple was the beginning of Jesus' deconstruction of the Jewish temple system. Consider the impact of:

1. His temple-like ministry—healing and forgiving people wherever He went.

    _____

    _____

2. His declaration to the woman of Samaria (John 4:21-24).

    _____

    _____

3. His second temple "cleansing"—the week before His crucifixion (Matthew 21:12-16).

    _____

    _____

4. His death—and the destruction of the temple services (Matthew 27:45-56).

    _____

    _____

5. His prophecy that the Temple would be totally destroyed (Matthew 24:1-3), which took place in AD 70.

    _____

    _____

6. His followers being the dwelling place (temple) of the Holy Spirit (1 Corinthians 3:16, 6:19).

    _____

    _____

REFLECTION

In reflecting on the Scriptures and insights in this guide, what struck you as new or important?

_____

_____

What got Jesus passionate—even angry? Do you get passionate about the same things?

_____

_____

Jesus' Kingdom movement is not about buildings. Christian faith is not to be building focused. How does this compare with your church experience?

_____

_____

How are you making Jesus central to life each day?

_____

_____

SHARING

What will you share with friends on this journey with you?

_____

_____

What will you share with those you are encouraging to be disciples of Jesus?

_____

_____

MEETING NICODEMUS

A Member of the Jewish Council

JESUS WAS A JEW, as were His first disciples, but His actions and words undermined the temple system. He claimed to be a one-man temple—and went about doing temple work: healing and forgiving.[1] John records that "many people saw the miraculous signs that he was doing and believed in his name" (John 2:23), then shares four stories: the first being an interview with a Pharisee, Nicodemus, "a member of the ruling Jewish council" (John 3:1).

READ
- John 3:1-21
- *Messiah*, chapter 17

What was disturbing Nicodemus? Why did he come under the cover of darkness (John 3:1-2)?

_____

_____

How did Jesus' response confront this Pharisee's view of the Kingdom (John 3:3)?

_____

_____

Jesus told Nicodemus, a religious leader, that he needed to be reborn to see the Kingdom of God. From their conversation (John 3:4-21), what view did Nicodemus have of the Kingdom of God?

_____

_____

How did Jesus' view of the Kingdom of God differ?

_____

_____

VIEWS OF THE KINGDOM

There were a variety of interest groups, each with their own ideas of kingdom:[2]

- Sadducees were a priestly temple aristocracy, a conservative religious party with political clout, who accepted only the written law of Moses as authoritative.

- Pharisees were influential, nonclerical Jews who thought that by pursuing every detail of the whole Torah law, they could hasten the day when God would rescue Israel from pagan domination.[3]

- Essenes, known for their retreat in the wilderness at Qumran, were the third of the Torah Schools with substantial influence in Jerusalem in Jesus' time.[4]

- Zealots were frustrated by lack of action, committed to violent resistance to achieve their vision of the kingdom of Israel restored, and prepared to fight the Romans.

- Herodians supported compromise, backing the Herods to achieve their ends and convinced the Zealots were out of their minds to think they could overthrow the Romans.

- The ruling Jewish Council, called the Sanhedrin, governed daily Jewish life. The Roman Empire ruled Israel through the appointed provincial governor, who collected taxes, extended roads, defended borders, and provided produce for Rome, but the Sanhedrin ruled the lives of the Jews. It also acted as a court but could not condemn a person to death for sedition. Chaired by the high priest, Pharisees were well represented on the council, but Sadducees dominated. No secular Jew could serve.

All had a tribal view of God, believing His Kingdom was for Jews only! But Jesus' message was radically different. He challenged Nicodemus with an alternative view of God and kingdom.

Jesus used a familiar story from Jewish history to illustrate that entry to God's Kingdom is by faith—for "everyone who believes." How did Jesus apply this (John 3:14-18, compare Numbers 21:4-9)?

_____

_____

What was Jesus' "verdict" (John 3:19-21)?

_____

_____

What was Jesus saying about Himself (John 3:4-21)?

_____

_____

MORE ABOUT NICODEMUS

John mentions Nicodemus two more times. What do we learn from these brief encounters?

- John 7:50:

_____

_____

- John 19:38-42:

_____

_____

REFLECTION

In what ways did Jesus' conversation with Nicodemus affirm the radical nonsectarian nature of God's Kingdom?

_____

_____

SHARING

What is Jesus saying to you about new birth in the story of Nicodemus?

_____

_____

What will you share with friends you are leading to Jesus?

_____

_____

EXPLOSIVE GROWTH

More Disciples than John

FROM JESUS' *ministry foundation* phase of disciplemaking, following His declaration that He was the temple, John tells four stories. There was Jesus' night meeting with Nicodemus in Jerusalem, then His multiplying movement in the hills of Judea, a journey through Samaria, and the healing of a Roman official's son in Galilee. These illustrate the scope and nature of Jesus' Kingdom and temple ministry.

READ
- John 3:22–4:3
- *Messiah*, chapter 18

Jesus moved to Judea, where His disciple-making movement was marked by explosive growth, causing concern to some of John's disciples. What was John's reaction?

_____

_____

What did John model for his disciples and us?

_____

_____

What did John say was his "source of real joy"?[1] What lessons can we learn from John the Baptist?

_____

_____

In *Knowing Him*, Mark Edwards notes three characteristics of John as a man of God:

1. He knew who he was—and who Jesus was.
2. His joy came from being next to the "Bridegroom"—and hearing Him.
3. He knew that once he heard Jesus, "he could do nothing but obey."

"John is one of the clearest pictures of a man who has learned to die to self and live to Christ. He found the source of real joy in Jesus."[2]

What could it mean to decrease to allow Jesus to increase in your life?

_____

_____

How are you cultivating the priority of being with Jesus, listening to Him, and obeying?

_____

_____

What are hindrances in your daily routine that prevent you from spending time with Jesus?

_____

_____

John had moved to the river Aenon, on the borders of Samaria. He had been preparing the way for Jesus among Jews, but now he was near Samaria. Why was he there?

_____

_____

Why had John not ended his ministry to follow Jesus, as he told his disciples to do?

_____

_____

Reread John 3:27-36. What is the attitude of a real disciple?

_____

_____

Is it possible that Jesus had asked John to continue preparing the way? As Jesus established the foundations for His ministry, was John to move to the borders of Samaria to prepare the way for His ministry there also? Had Jesus and John had these discussions?

What was Jesus modeling in John 4:1-3?

_____

_____

Where was Jesus planning to go next?

_____

_____

REFLECTION

What has been fresh or new to you in this guide?

_____

_____

Many were becoming followers of Jesus. What attracts you to following Him? What are the obstacles?

_____

_____

SHARING

What will you share with friends who are on this journey with you?

_____

_____

What will you share with those you are encouraging to know Jesus better?

_____

_____

A SAMARITAN WOMAN

Conversing with a Despised Relative

IF JESUS WAS to deliver Israel from Roman bondage, an interview with a member of the Jewish ruling council seemed appropriate, but to visit with Samaritans was entirely out of order. Jews hated them more than the Romans. Avoiding the coastal Via Maris, traversed by Roman soldiers, most Jews chose the longer Jordan Valley road rather than travel through the towns of these religious and political enemies. Yet Jesus took His disciples through Samaria. A Samaritan woman would be the first to hear Him declare Himself the Messiah.

READ
- John 4:1-42
- *Messiah*, chapter 19

What prompted this trip (John 4:1-4)?

_____

_____

Jesus was attracting attention. Why might this have been a problem?

_____

_____

Jesus left Judea, moving north into Galilee. Herod Antipas, of Perea and Galilee, was less than pleased with John the Baptist's preaching. When John rebuked him for taking Herodias, his brother Philip's wife (tetrarch of Trachonitis), Antipas locked John up, silencing him (Matthew 14:3-5; Luke 3:19-20, compare Mark 1:14). Jesus moved to Galilee, continuing the movement John had begun.

John records that Jesus "had to go through Samaria." Why this imperative?

_____

_____

THE SAMARITANS

As far as most Jews were concerned, Samaritans definitely had no place in a restored Jewish kingdom! There was a long history of bad blood between them. Samaritans shared a common ancestry: part Jew, part Egyptian (the descendants of Ephraim and Manasseh).[1] What is more, they had intermarried with the Assyrians. Thus, the Jews considered them racially inferior, "half-breeds"—not Jews at all. They would bow down to pagan deities, and a common Jewish saying was that "he that eats the bread of a Samaritan is like to one that eats the flesh of swine."[2] It is summed up well in the words: "Jews do not associate with Samaritans" (John 4:9).

Try to imagine the scene: Jesus and the Samaritan woman meeting at Jacob's Well. What do you picture (John 4:5-9)?

_____

_____

It was noon. Jesus was alone and exhausted. He sat "on the well" (John 4:6, KJV). A capstone in the shape of a "large donut," eighteen inches to two feet thick and about five feet across, with a hole in the center, provided a working platform over such wells. The well was 130 feet deep, with no bucket attached.[3]

It took ten minutes to walk from Sychar (in Nablus today)—and the woman came alone.

_____

_____

Imagine the unease: Jesus was expected to step back twenty to twenty-three feet to allow the woman to approach the well, unroll her small leather bucket, draw water, fill her jar, and leave. But Jesus deliberately sat on the well, without a bucket.[4] Why didn't He move?

_____

_____

Jesus broke the uncomfortable silence with a simple request. But to engage this woman in conversation violated one of the most well-kept Jewish rules, that a man should not speak with a woman not his wife or close relative in public—and she was a Samaritan. What was her reaction?

_____

_____

How did Jesus lead this woman to be a disciple? Can you identify the five invitations of Jesus: "Come and see"; "Follow me"; "Fish with me"; "Love your enemy"; and "Receive the Spirit" (John 4:10-26)?

_____

_____

What indication is there of Jesus' sensitivity to this woman (verses 10-12)?

_____

_____

How did Jesus respond to her cynicism (verses 13-14)?

_____

_____

In her response, what indicates her heart need (verse 15)?

_____

_____

Jesus invited her to include her family in her spiritual journey, resulting in a seemingly superficial theological discussion. How did Jesus turn this into an opportunity to redefine her understanding of God and religion (verses 16-24)?

_____

_____

What declaration did Jesus make, in response to the woman's comment that the Messiah "is coming" (verses 25-26)?

_____

_____

What parallels do you find in Jesus' deconstruction of the temple (John 2:13-22) and what He said to this woman?

_____

_____

"Just then [Jesus'] disciples returned and were *surprised* to find him talking with a woman. But no one asked, 'What do you want?' or 'Why are you talking with her?'" (John 4:27, emphasis added). She left hurriedly, maybe embarrassed by them, but by the time she arrived in Sychar she called: "Come, see a man who told me everything I ever did. Could this be the Christ?" (John 4:28-29).

While she was gone, Jesus addressed four spiritual flaws common in disciples. How do you relate to His comments—or silence—regarding these?

- *Prejudice* (John 4:27):

_____

_____

- *Preoccupation* (John 4:31-34):

_____

_____

- *Preconditions* (John 4:35):

_____

_____

- *Pride* (John 4:36-38):

_____

_____

Then the woman returned with many from the town who now believed in him because of the woman's testimony. They urged Jesus and the disciples to stay—"and he stayed two days. And because of his words many more became believers" (John 4:40-41). How uncomfortable might the Jewish disciples have been? What lessons were they getting?

_____

_____

What conclusion did the townspeople come to (John 4:42)?

_____

_____

This story illustrates the countercultural nature of Jesus' idea of kingdom, as well as how He made disciples!

SAVIOR OF THE WORLD

Herod the Great rebuilt the city of Samaria (calling it Sebaste) with a temple, seen on a clear day from the Mediterranean port of Caesarea, dedicated to honor and flatter his Roman overlord, Caesar Augustus.

Greek and Roman rulers had taken the title *sōter* (*savior*) and Augustus, who died in AD 14, had been deified. Yet, after two days talking with Jesus, with the Caesar's huge statue a short distance away, the Samaritans declared of Jesus: "We know that this man really is the Savior of the world" (John 4:42).[5]

CHRIST'S METHOD OF DISCIPLEMAKING

There is no movement without disciplemaking, and Jesus' approach is the most effective: "Christ's method alone will give true success in reaching the people. The Savior mingled with men as one who desired their good. He showed His sympathy for them, ministered to their needs, and won their confidence. Then He told them, 'Follow Me.'"[6] His invitations demonstrate a five-step process:

Process	Invitations	Nature of Invitations
1. Connect	"Come and see"	Experiential
2. Engage	"Follow me"	Relational
3. Involve–build	"Fish with me"	Participatory
4. Equip	"Love your enemies"	Sacrificial
5. Send–multiply	"Receive the Spirit"	Empowered

REFLECTION

What have you enjoyed most about observing Jesus' relationship with the woman of Samaria?

_____

_____

SHARING

From this story, what will you share with your friends?

_____

_____

What will you share, and how will you now relate, with those you are encouraging to know Jesus better?

_____

_____

A ROYAL OFFICIAL

Healing for Gentiles

JESUS IS MOVING from His early Judean ministry back to Galilee. During this *ministry foundation* time, He went to Jerusalem, removed the sacrificial animals necessary for forgiveness and healing, declared He was the temple—then began doing temple ministry among the people. His ministry encompassed Jerusalem, Judea, Samaria, and now Galilee: Jews, Samaritans, and Gentiles.

READ
- John 4:43-54; Luke 4:14-15
- *Messiah*, chapter 20

News of events in Jerusalem had already reached Galilee, and the pepole there welcomed and praised Jesus. How would you think people in Nazareth felt about these reports?

_____

_____

Being back in Galilee, Jesus revisited Cana, where He had shown His glory to family and disciples. While He was there, a royal official arrived from Capernaum, asking Jesus to intervene for his dying son. What do we know about this man?

_____

_____

Reflect on the royal official's response: "The man took Jesus at his word and departed" (John 4:50). How did he know Jesus could heal?

_____

_____

Imagine the meeting of the official with his servants, halfway between Cana and Capernaum—the relief, the excitement! Try to picture the official asking for "the time when his son got better," when the realization swept over them that it was at "the exact time" Jesus had said: "Your son will live" (John 4:51-53)! What might have been the impact of this realization?

_____

_____

This was Jesus' "second miraculous sign" (John 4:54). Not only was the son of the royal official healed, but he and "all his household believed" (John 4:53). This miracle prepared the way for Jesus' multiplying ministry in Capernaum, as we will see. This official was a *person of peace* preparing the way for Jesus in his *oikos*—or extended family—in the region of Galilee and beyond.

CONSIDERING "FAITH"

Explore the meaning of faith by reading Hebrews 11:1-40:

In your own words, how do you define faith?

_____

_____

Why is it "impossible to please God" (Hebrews 11:6) without faith?

_____

_____

Do any of these stories of faith trouble you? Why?

_____

_____

Which of these faith stories do you personally find most encouraging?

_____

_____

How do you understand Hebrews 11:39-40?

_____

_____

How do you go about living "by faith, not by sight" (2 Corinthians 5:7)?

_____

_____

GALILEE

The Sea of Galilee was also called "Sea of Kinnereth"—maybe from the Hebrew *kinnor* or harp because of its shape.[1] It was also called the "Lake of Gennesaret," with the plain of Gennesaret on its northwest shores, and the "Sea of Tiberias," after the new city built on its southwestern shores by Herod Antipas. Being fed by the Jordan River with fresh water from the Golan Heights, it was 660 feet below sea level, sixteen miles long, and nine miles wide. It sustained a thriving fishing industry in the days of Jesus.

Upper Galilee was to the north and west of the lake, a mountainous area rising 3300 feet above sea level, a natural boundary with Phoenicia, which is Lebanon today. Lower Galilee was the area around the lake, a fertile agricultural area about 590 feet below sea level, with many towns and villages.

Since the Assyrian invasion of the northern kingdom of Israel in the days of Isaiah, the population of this area was mixed: strongly Jewish but with Gentiles among them. It was on the Via Maris, the main trading road connecting Mesopotamia and Damascus with Egypt and Africa. This was the "way of the sea" (Isaiah 9:1), which passed through Capernaum on the northern shore of the Sea of Galilee.

The border with the territory of Gaulanitis to the northwest was the Jordan flowing into the sea. Bethsaida—hometown of Peter, Andrew, and

Philip—was just across the river in that Gentile land. Capernaum was therefore a border town, a great place for tax collectors like Levi Matthew. Peter Walker raises the possibility that Peter and Andrew might have moved to Capernaum to avoid paying tax when transporting fish to towns on the western shores.[2] Across the sea to the east and southeast was the Gentile Roman region of Decapolis, or "ten cities."

Jesus' move to Capernaum was strategic. Isaiah prophesied that the Lord would "honor Galilee of the Gentiles, by the way of the sea" and that those living there would see a "great light" (Isaiah 9:1-2). He arrived with the message of a new kingdom—the Kingdom of God. Thirty years before Jesus' ministry in this region, the Galileans rebelled against Rome and failed; thirty years later they would try and fail again. Jesus arrived, declaring they could trust Him![3]

REFLECTION
What has been a fresh insight for you in this story?

_____

_____

What has Jesus done for you? And in what way have you chosen to welcome (John 4:45) Him into your life—your family, home, study, or workplace?

_____

_____

SHARING
What will you share with friends on this journey with you?

_____

_____

What will you share with those you are encouraging to follow Jesus?

_____

_____

ESSENTIAL FRAMES OF JESUS' MOVEMENT BUILDING

IT IS TIME to reflect on Jesus' journey up to this point. We have explored the *preparation* and *ministry foundation* years. We want to know Him, to experience the environment of His life and ministry, to identify with His struggles and movement building, and to incorporate His frames of movement building into our contexts and circumstances.

REFLECTION

How has your life been changed by walking with Jesus through the first eighteen months of His ministry, the ministry foundation phase?

_____

_____

What have you learned about Jesus?

_____

_____

What have you come to appreciate most about Him?

_____

_____

Has the direction of His ministry disturbed you? If so, in what ways?

_____

_____

ESSENTIAL FRAMES FROM JESUS' *MINISTRY FOUNDATIONS* PHASE

Review these and assess their importance to the Kingdom movement Jesus was building:

Jesus' five invitations:

_____

_____

Jesus' reliance on Holy Spirit POWER:

_____

_____

Jesus' movement encompassed all people:

_____

_____

Jesus' message is His method—a journey of descent for us:

_____

_____

Jesus is the new temple:

_____

_____

Suggest other things you have learned from this phase of Jesus' ministry:

_____

_____

How do these expand the essential features or priorities of the first (or *preparation*) phase of Jesus' life and movement building? These included:

The person: Jesus.

_____

_____

The principle: Status reversal.

_____

_____

The purpose: To do the Father's will.

_____

_____

The person of peace: Key in relational streams.

_____

_____

What do you think of the idea that Jesus came to both save and model disciplemaking, leading people to God and His Kingdom?

_____

_____

REFLECTION

In what way has this ministry foundation phase impacted you?

_____

_____

How has God convicted you, and for what purpose?

_____

_____

In what way is your life being changed by Jesus' foundational priorities?

_____

_____

How have you chosen to follow Jesus daily?

_____

_____

SHARING

What will you share with your friends who are on this journey with you?

_____

_____

As a result of exploring the preparation and ministry foundation phases of Jesus' life and disciplemaking, how are you now relating to those you are encouraging to know and follow Jesus as disciples?

_____

_____

Participation

EQUIPPING FOR EXPANDED OUTREACH

IN THE THIRD PHASE of Jesus' ministry, He was on the move. A new season had come, a new phase of His movement building. While the exact sequence of events might be debated, His transition to *equipping for expanded outreach* was marked by the imprisonment of His cousin John the Baptist and His own move from Judea to Galilee. This move was to fulfill His Father's purpose: a new hometown, a new political and cultural environment, a new ministry emphasis now that John was silenced, with new opportunities for expanding the Kingdom movement of God—with a new invitation!

This time of training for expanded outreach took about nine months—the last half of His second year of ministry and the first part of His third year. While the disciples being drawn into closer fellowship for training included some of the twelve apostles, Jesus did not choose the twelve until the end of this training.

This period covers sections 37–52 of *The NIV Harmony of the Gospels* and chapters 21–29 of Jerry Thomas' *Messiah*. These sections include the transition events: John's imprisonment; Jesus' visit and rejection in His hometown of Nazareth; His move to Capernaum; as well as a visit to Jerusalem, where He healed a man at the Bethesda pool, resulting in rejection by Jerusalem's religious leaders. They also cover His invitation to *fish*, together with the training received on seven *fishing trips*. This phase of Jesus' disciplemaking and movement building is hands-on, informative, and enriching.

ON THE MOVE

Major Transitions

JESUS' EIGHTEEN-MONTH ministry in Judea came to an abrupt end with the imprisonment of His cousin and friend, John the Baptist, an attempt to kill Him in His hometown Nazareth, and rejection in Jerusalem. While the situation appeared bleak, it gave an opportunity for Jesus to draw His followers closer, for them to join Him as apprentices in the school of disciplemaking, and for Him to teach them the process and equip them to multiply His movement.

READ
- Matthew 4:12-17; Mark 1:14-15; Luke 4:14-30
- *Messiah*, chapters 22–24

The transition to Jesus' third phase of movement building—a time of equipping for *participation* and *expanded outreach*—included:

IMPRISONMENT OF HIS COUSIN
How would Jesus have felt when He learned of this (Matthew 4:12-16)?

_____

_____

Why do you think Jesus chose Galilee?

_____

_____

How had prophets described this region (Matthew 4:12-17; compare Isaiah 9:1-2)?

_____

_____

TENSIONS IN JERUSALEM

Jesus' return to Jerusalem for a "feast of the Jews" (John 5:1), where He healed an invalid at the pool of Bethesda, might have taken place about this time. Some see the reaction of Jerusalem's hierarchy as a reason for Jesus' move to Galilee. Others place this visit later, just before the appointment of the twelve apostles. Our next guide will examine this story in greater detail.

Read John 5:1-47. What accusations were made against Jesus, and how did He respond?

_____

_____

ATTEMPT TO KILL HIM

What were the reactions to Jesus' comments in the synagogue of His hometown of Nazareth (Luke 4:14-30)?

_____

_____

How did Jesus define His life and ministry by the prophecy of Isaiah 61:1-2?

_____

_____

Compare Luke 4:18-19 with Isaiah 61:1-2—and note the section He omitted. Why do you think Jesus did not read the full passage?

_____

_____

How do you understand Jesus' explanation in verses 24-27?

_____

_____

Why do you think the Jews of His hometown were so incensed, so enraged that they wanted to kill Him?

_____

_____

Jesus escaped to Capernaum (Luke 4:31), a fishing town of about 1500 people with a tax station, a Roman garrison of 100 soldiers, but with no paved streets, sewer system, running water, or theater.[1] Considering the political, social, and religious environment of "Galilee of the Gentiles," what opportunities did Capernaum offer for His developing movement (Matthew 4:12-16, compare Isaiah 9:1)?

_____

_____

With His cousin silenced, it was time for Jesus to step forward as leader of the movement. Why did Jesus take up John's message? And did He suggest a new emphasis (Matthew 3:1-2, 4:17, compare Mark 1:14-15)?

_____

_____

REFLECTION

Jesus moved His base to "the land of the nations" (Matthew 4:15). He took up John's message, repositioned Himself as movement leader, and issued a more demanding call for His team.

How have you coped with major loss and setbacks (even rejection) in life?

_____

_____

What might have been some of Jesus' thoughts and emotions during this time?

_____

_____

What were potential causes of derailment for His movement?

_____

_____

What have you learned from how Jesus related to the transitions in His life?

_____

_____

What transitions are needed for your ministry to become a movement?

_____

_____

SHARING

What will you share with friends who are on this journey with you?

_____

_____

What will you share with those you are encouraging to know and follow Jesus?

_____

_____

HEALING AT BETHESDA POOL—
ON SABBATH!

IN THIS GUIDE, we revisit Jerusalem with Jesus. You will recall what happened during His first Passover visit after His baptism. If the feast of John 5:1 was the second Passover He attended, it was now eighteen months since His baptism and twelve months since He drove out the animals of sacrifice and declared Himself to be the one-person temple. On this visit, He healed an invalid at the Pool of Bethesda on a Sabbath, provoking another major conflict with Jewish leaders—again, at the temple. The pool was near the sheep markets, just outside the city walls at the northern end of the Temple Mount.

READ
- John 5:1-47
- *Messiah*, chapter 21

What do you learn about the invalid (John 5:1-15)?

_____

_____

Why did Jesus ask the invalid, "Do you want to get well?" (John 5:6)

_____

_____

Try to imagine:

How did invalids care for themselves when there was no disability support system?

_____

_____

How would the life of this invalid of thirty-eight years change if he were made well?

_____

_____

If begging provided his income, what would the invalid do if healed? If he was the organizer of the disabled beside the Bethesda Pool, what would his healing mean in lost social networks?

_____

_____

Mark Edwards surmises that this invalid might have been "a crusty old con man," inventing the story of the moving waters (John 5:4, footnote reference) to gather unfortunate people to increase his takings.[1] *What do you think?*

_____

_____

John records no evidence of repentance, gratitude, or any expression of faith from this man. Why do you think this might have been?

_____

_____

When Jesus found the man at the Temple, why did Jesus say, "Stop sinning or something worse may happen to you" (John 5:14)?

_____

_____

JESUS, THE TEMPLE, AND SABBATH

Jesus met the healed man at the Temple, setting up another encounter with the Jewish leaders. Why were the Jews upset with the invalid and Jesus? What did they understand by Jesus' actions and attitude toward Sabbath (reread John 5:8-18)?

The Jews did not miss what Jesus was doing and saying. He had declared Himself to be the temple, and now He was claiming equality with God: doing God's work on Sabbath.

The Sabbath—Shabbat or Saturday—was instituted in creation before sin, and prior to the Jews or the giving of the law to Israel (Genesis 2:1-3). The Sabbath command is unique, the first positive command of the Ten Commandments and the only one that identifies God as the Creator:

> [God said,] "Remember the Sabbath day by keeping it holy. . . .
> For in six days the LORD made the heavens and the earth . . .
> but he rested on the seventh day. Therefore the LORD blessed the
> Sabbath day and made it holy."
> EXODUS 20:8-11

It was the gift of the Creator.

It also reminded Jews of their deliverance or salvation from Egyptian captivity (Deuteronomy 5:12-15). While a "sanctuary in time"[2] for believers—a reminder of the good news that there is no work that we can do to save ourselves (Hebrews 4:1-10)—the Jews had developed numerous burdensome regulations to guard this gift from God.

JESUS—IDENTITY AND TRUTH

Because He healed on the Sabbath, Jesus faced two charges:

1. He was accused of "breaking the Sabbath."
2. He was accused of "making himself equal with God."

His defense was to present the testimony of five witnesses. What do we learn about Jesus from these testimonies? Reread John 5:16-47:

- His own witness (John 5:19-31):

  _____

  _____

- John the Baptist's witness (John 5:31-35):

  _____

  _____

- His own works as a witness (John 5:36):

  _____

  _____

- His Father's witness (John 5:37-38, compare Matthew 3:13-17, at the Jordan):

  _____

  _____

- Scripture's witness (John 5:39-46):

  _____

  _____

Jesus was fully God and fully human, God made flesh. He presented Himself as the one-man temple, then defined Himself by the Sabbath as the Creator. He had created and made the Sabbath holy. It testified to His divinity!

Why do you think Jesus did this as He moved into a deeper level of ministry training and outreach in Galilee?

_____

_____

How do you see Jesus defining His movement by the temple and Sabbath?

_____

_____

Jesus disclosed His real identity. What were the implications for His disciples and His movement building?

_____

_____

REFLECTION

What was new for you in this section?

_____

_____

What does Jesus' identity as both truly God and fully human mean to you personally?

_____

_____

SHARING

What will you share with friends who are on this journey with you?

_____

_____

What did Jesus say about Himself? And how could you share this with friends who do not yet follow Jesus?

_____

_____

"COME FISH WITH ME"

Jesus Invites Participation

TEMPLE LEADERS in Jerusalem were intent on killing Him (John 5:16-18), as were at least some of the villagers of Nazareth (Luke 4:28-30). His cousin was in a dungeon at Machaerus, east of the Dead Sea. It was a time of change. A new phase of ministry had begun, and it was time to move forward in His disciplemaking. Jesus returned to His new home in Capernaum and went in search of some of His disciples on the shores of Galilee.

READ
- Matthew 4:18-22; Mark 1:16-20; Luke 5:1-11
- *Messiah*, chapter 25

Who did Jesus find? And what were they doing?

_____

_____

What was Jesus' invitation?

_____

_____

How did these disciples respond?

_____

_____

How long had Jesus known these men, and what experiences had they shared?

_____

_____

What were His first three invitations?

1. _____

    _____

2. _____

    _____

3. _____

    _____

How does His third invitation relate to the first two?

_____

_____

SOME CLARIFICATIONS

The missing stories: Matthew and Mark give the impression that Jesus moved straight from the wilderness temptations into Capernaum, to extend His invitation to fish for people. However, there were eighteen months of ministry between these two experiences. This *foundation* phase of Jesus' movement building is only found in John's Gospel. It was a time of significant growth when the foundations were laid for His movement. Both Matthew and Mark pinpoint the imprisonment of John the Baptist as the time when Jesus moved to Galilee.

The misleading title: The NIV section heading for Matthew 4:18-22 is "Jesus Calls His First Disciples." This is misleading, for His first call was given at Bethany-beyond-Jordan. He had invested His life in many already (John 3:22). Now, Jesus was moving forward in His disciple-making, extending a third invitation.

The invitation was not to employment: These men had businesses, work, and families (Mark 1:20; Luke 4:38, 5:10). Jesus had already invested time with them and others. He had visited Capernaum with His mother and brothers after the wedding in Cana (John 2:12). Peter would have talked over following Jesus with his wife and mother-in-law; James and John with their father Zebedee and, perhaps, with their mother. This family became strong supporters and partners of Jesus' movement. But the invitations Jesus gave in making disciples should not be confused with employment or a religious vocation. Jesus did not offer that!

INVITATION 3: "FISH WITH ME"

Why do you think Jesus issued this more demanding call to on-the-job training and participation in His expanding movement?

_____

_____

In what ways might this new invitation contribute to the expansion of Jesus' movement?

_____

_____

These disciples left behind family and business to go "fishing" with Jesus. But also compare Matthew 4:18-22 and Mark 1:16-20 with Luke 5:1-11. What evidence do you find that Luke is telling of a later "calling"? Note these aspects of the reports:

- The sequence:

  _____

- The disciples' activities:

  _____

  _____

- The activities of Jesus:

  _____

  _____

- The catch of fish:

  _____

  _____

If Luke's account is of another call to "fish" for people—given after Jesus' tour of Galilee (Matthew 4:23-25; Mark 1:35-39; Luke 4:42-44), where I think it fits—it indicates their association with Jesus was *on the path of everyday life*. He equipped them to *fish for people* while at the same time they engaged in their vocations as fishermen on the Sea of Galilee. This is where disciplemaking happens today!

What "good things" might need to be left behind for the mission of Jesus?

_____

_____

How could this be negotiated with family and business associates?

_____

_____

What are the advantages of fishing with Jesus in your current vocation?

_____

_____

How might you know whether and when to enter an employed religious vocation?

_____

_____

In what ways could your present vocation be described as full-time ministry?

_____

_____

REFLECTION

What impact do you think it had for Jesus to go to the workplace of these fishermen to call them to participate in disciplemaking with Him?

_____

_____

What do you find most exciting—and scariest—about the invitation to participate in making disciples?

_____

_____

SHARING

Jesus had been watching these four fishermen. They had traveled with Him. They were disciples. He moved to Galilee to invest more in them, to equip them as disciplemakers. Who are you investing your life in?

_____

_____

Discuss with your friends how you are investing in others, as Jesus did.

_____

_____

With those you are encouraging to follow Jesus, share the idea of investing their lives in others. Who are they investing their lives in?

_____

_____

FISHING WITH JESUS

Trips One through Four

JESUS WAS GOD and human. Although it is unlikely the disciples fully understood the import of His claims concerning the Temple or Sabbath, it was dawning on them that Jesus was no ordinary person. Peter and "all" his fellow fishermen were "astonished at the catch of fish" they took when Jesus was around. They were ready to follow when He said, "Don't be afraid; from now on you will catch men" (Luke 5:1-11).

Jesus had already invested time in them. They had shared many *experiences* together. They, their families, and their work associates had a growing *relationship* with Him—and it was now time to *participate* in training for expanded ministry.

Jesus took them *fishing*, demonstrating how to reach people with the good news that He was the Messiah. Mark Edwards observes, "There is progression to these fishing trips, a good pattern for us to follow, and much to learn about fishing for [people]."[1] Edwards uses four key questions to look at these outreach events, and we will use the same:

1. Where is Jesus fishing?
2. Who is Jesus fishing for?
3. What is Jesus modeling in each situation?
4. How is Jesus fishing?

Building on these questions, Edwards also proposes three questions by which to evaluate evangelistic events:[2]

1. Were there nonbelievers at the event?
2. Was Jesus presented clearly in a culturally relevant way as the Messiah or Savior of the world?
3. Did anyone believe and put their faith in Jesus for salvation or move closer to accepting His claims to be the Messiah?

We will adapt these to evaluate each experience.

READ
- Mark 1:21-38; Luke 4:31-44; compare Matthew 8:14-17
- *Messiah*, chapter 26

TRIP ONE: IN A SYNAGOGUE—A RELIGIOUS CENTER (MARK 1:21-28; LUKE 4:31-37)

Where was Jesus fishing?

_____

_____

Who was Jesus fishing for?

_____

_____

What did Jesus model in this religious setting?

_____

_____

How was Jesus fishing?

_____

_____

How did He start in this religious setting (Mark 1:21; Luke 4:31)?

_____

_____

What did the demon say about Jesus, and why did Jesus silence the demon?

_____

_____

Why were people amazed at His teaching (Mark 1:22, 27; Luke 4:32, 36)?

_____

_____

Evaluation: How Did Jesus and His Disciples Do?

Were there nonbelievers present?

_____

_____

How did Jesus present Himself in a culturally relevant way as Messiah and Savior?

_____

_____

Who put their faith in Him or moved closer to accepting Him as Messiah?

_____

_____

Application

What religious setting might God be calling you to connect with?

_____

_____

TRIP TWO: IN A HOUSE—PETER'S HOME (MATTHEW 8:14-17; MARK 1:29-34; LUKE 4:38-41)

Where was Jesus fishing?

_____

_____

Who was Jesus fishing for?

_____

_____

What did Jesus model in this home?

_____

_____

How was Jesus fishing?

_____

_____

How did this evening of ministry begin (Mark 1:29-31; Luke 4:38-39)?

_____

_____

What did the demons recognize (Mark 1:32-34; Luke 4:40-41)?

_____

_____

Evaluation: How Did Jesus and His Disciples Do?
Were there nonbelievers present?

_____

_____

How did Jesus present Himself in a culturally relevant way as Messiah and Savior?

_____

_____

Who put their faith in Him or moved closer to accepting Him as Messiah?

_____

_____

Application
How could you connect with the needs and share with those in your home or immediate neighborhood?

_____

_____

What might the impact of this be for you and your family?

_____

_____

TRIP THREE: IN THEIR REGION—A SHORT TOUR OF GALILEE (MARK 1:35-39; LUKE 4:42-44; COMPARE MATTHEW 4:23-25)

Where was Jesus fishing?

_____

_____

Who was Jesus fishing for?

_____

_____

What did Jesus model on this tour?

_____

_____

How was Jesus fishing?

_____

_____

Why do you think it was important for Jesus to take some disciples to other towns and villages?

_____

_____

What was the impact of this tour (Matthew 4:24-25)?

_____

_____

Evaluation: How Did Jesus and His Disciples Do?

Were there nonbelievers present?

_____

_____

How did Jesus present Himself in a culturally relevant way as Messiah and Savior?

_____

_____

Who put their faith in Him or moved closer to accepting Him as Messiah?

_____

_____

Application

In following His Father's plan, what did Jesus do to prepare for this tour?

_____

_____

What short-term mission trip could you and your friends plan? When will you do this?

_____

_____

TRIP FOUR: IN A PUBLIC PLACE—BESIDE THE SEA (LUKE 5:1-11)

Where was Jesus fishing?

_____

_____

Who was Jesus fishing for?

_____

_____

What did Jesus model on this occasion?

_____

_____

How was Jesus fishing?

_____

_____

How did Jesus focus all the people on the point of His teaching (Luke 5:4-10)?

_____

_____

What did Simon Peter conclude (Luke 5:8-10)?

_____

_____

Evaluation: How Did Jesus and His Disciples Do?

Were there nonbelievers present?

_____

_____

How did Jesus present Himself in a culturally relevant way as Messiah and Savior?

_____

_____

Who put their faith in Him or moved closer to accepting Him as Messiah?

_____

_____

Application

Rather than trying to assemble a crowd, Jesus went to the people. What might this mean in planning your outreach event?

_____

_____

We read that "they pulled their boats up on shore, left everything and followed him" (Luke 5:11). Remember, Jesus was not offering employment, so what did this mean? What could this mean for you?

_____

_____

SHARING

With your friends, settle on a time and place where you will be involved in outreach.

_____

_____

How could you involve the friends you are inviting to follow Jesus?

_____

_____

FISHING WITH JESUS

Trips Five and Six

THE LOCATIONS for the first fishing trips were identified, but for the next three, the focus was the desperate need of the people. These also resulted in dramatic multiplication for Jesus' movement. We look at two trips in this guide and, in the next, explore how Jesus worked to lead a tax collector to be a disciple, one who He would appoint as one of His twelve apostles. These are amazing stories with specific lessons for our disciplemaking.

READ
- Matthew 8:1-13; Mark 1:40–2:12; Luke 5:12-26
- *Messiah*, chapter 27

TRIP FIVE: A LEPER (LUKE 5:12-16)

Where was Jesus fishing?

_____

_____

Who was Jesus fishing for?

_____

_____

What did Jesus model in this unnamed town?

_____

_____

A man covered with leprosy was an outcast. The priests, "the keepers of the public health of the community, had the responsibility to protect the people from the spread of this disease."[1] In Leviticus 13, God gave detailed instructions to the priests on how to assess skin disease, and if found to be infectious, the person "must wear torn clothes, let his hair be unkempt, cover the lower part of his face and cry out, 'Unclean! Unclean!'" The Levitical law was clear: "As long as he has the infection he remains unclean. He must live alone; he must live outside the camp" (Leviticus 13:45-46). Outcast, unloved, socially rejected, feared, the leper had to live away from loved ones and their touch!

How was Jesus fishing?

_____

_____

What was the significance of Jesus touching this man with an infectious disease?

_____

_____

In Leviticus 14:1-32, instructions were also given concerning the priest's involvement and sacrifices to be made when there was healing. In light of Jesus' claim to be the one temple—the One bringing healing and forgiveness—why would He have told the leper to tell no one and go to the priest?

_____

_____

Evaluation: How Did Jesus and His Disciples Do?

Were there nonbelievers present?

_____

_____

How did Jesus present Himself in a culturally relevant way as Messiah and Savior?

_____

_____

Who put their faith in Him or moved closer to accepting Him as Messiah?

_____

_____

Application

What has been your experience as an outcast, touched and cleansed by Jesus?

_____

_____

We are to fish for lepers. Who are the outcasts you know—perhaps some you treat as lepers? Identify them:

_____

_____

What was the impact of this fishing expedition on Jesus' movement building (Luke 5:15)?

_____

_____

Amid the clamor of the crowds, where did Jesus find direction for His movement (Luke 5:16)?

_____

_____

Jesus' disciple-making movement was now getting out of control. He gave a "strong warning" to the leper to tell no one, but "instead [the leper] went out and began to talk freely, spreading the news. As a result, Jesus could no longer enter a town openly but stayed outside in lonely places. Yet the people still came to him from everywhere" (Mark 1:43, 45).

TRIP SIX: A PARALYTIC (LUKE 5:17-26; MARK 2:1-12)

Where was Jesus fishing (compare Matthew 9:1 with Mark 2:1)?

_____

_____

How was Jesus fishing?

_____

_____

Who was Jesus fishing for (Luke 5:17)?

_____

_____

What part might the healing of the leper have had in bringing this group together?

_____

_____

The room was crowded. What might they have been talking about?

_____

_____

In what way did the arrival of the paralytic through the roof provide a great illustration of the relationship between Jesus and His Father?

_____

_____

What did Jesus model, and what lessons were the disciples learning . . .

- About Jesus?

_____

- About making disciples?

_____

_____

Mark Edwards observes that the paralytic had "incredible friends" who "got creative in doing whatever it took to get their friend to Jesus." He then asks, "Do you love anyone enough to do whatever it takes to get him/her to Jesus?"[2]

Evaluation: How Did Jesus and His Disciples Do?

Were there nonbelievers present?

_____

_____

How did Jesus present Himself in a culturally relevant way as Messiah and Savior?

_____

_____

Who put their faith in Him or moved closer to accepting Him as Messiah?

_____

_____

Application

What was the response of all in the room (compare Luke 5:26 with verse 17)?

_____

_____

Jesus' disciple-making movement was now impacting Pharisees and teachers of the law.

SHARING

Who do you know who is an outcast—a spiritual leper?

_____

_____

Who do you know who is spiritually paralyzed, who needs their sins forgiven?

_____

_____

With your friends, follow Jesus' example:

- Choose one of the fishing expeditions of Jesus as a model. Spend time praying and settle on the time and place where you will share:

_____

_____

How could you involve your friends who are themselves coming to know Jesus be involved in a "fishing expedition" with you?

_____

_____

FISHING WITH JESUS

Trip Seven

CONSIDERING THE TIME Jesus invested in people, His call to Levi Matthew to "follow" and then, within weeks, to be appointed as one of the twelve apostles, seems somewhat out of character. But, what do we learn from this story of Jesus' movement building? And how does this story illustrate what Jesus was doing: moving the fences of expectation, redefining the boundaries of the Kingdom, and establishing His movement on a sacrificial, selfless, altruistic worldview?

This story is part of the transition into the next phase of Jesus' ministry: *leadership multiplication*. There will be more Sabbath controversies, and then Jesus moves into the most challenging phase of disciplemaking and movement building: the transformation of worldview!

READ
- Matthew 9:9-17; Mark 2:13-22; Luke 5:27-39
- *Messiah*, chapter 28

TRIP SEVEN: A TAX COLLECTOR (LUKE 5:27-32)
Where was Jesus fishing?

_____

_____

Who was Jesus fishing for?

What did Jesus model in this situation?

TAX COLLECTORS IN GALILEE

Matthew was a tax collector at Capernaum on the northwestern shores of Galilee, only about 2 miles from the borders of Gaulanitis, the territory of the tetrarch Philip. About 7.5 miles south, overlooking the lake, was Tiberias, where Herod Antipas, with his *messianic* aspirations, extracted crushing taxes from the people. At Magdala in between (the hometown of Mary Magdalene), the stench of the fish-processing factory—one of Herod Antipas's moneymaking machines—filled the town.[1]

The peasants of Galilee suffered harsh economic and social dislocation. The Romans occupied their land. Three decades before Jesus' birth, Herod the Great courted Emperor Augustus to become client king over Judea and Galilee, a rule of "splendor and terror." To fund his lavish lifestyle, extensive building projects, and gifts for the Emperor, he imposed an impossible tax burden on his subjects. Posing as a "new Solomon," he rebuilt the Jewish temple—making it a wonder of the world.

When Herod the Great died in 4 BC, his son Archelaus became his successor. He had little sense of Jewish feelings and when confronted with rebellious temple pilgrims, he mobilized his cavalry, killing thousands. In the uprisings that followed, the son of a Galilean bandit who had been executed by Herod the Great years earlier led a rampage through Sepphoris, administrative capital of Galilee, about a forty-five-minute walk from Nazareth. Rome reacted, sweeping through Galilean villages, raping, killing, destroying—and razing Sepphoris.

In the aftermath of these uprisings, the sixth son of Herod the Great, Antipas—only sixteen at the time and studying in Rome—argued before Emperor Augustus that he should be primary heir. His elder brother Archelaus was demoted to "ethnarch" (communal leader) over Judea, Samaria, and Idumea; his next brother, Philip, was made "tetrarch" (territorial leader) of modern Golan, northern Israel and Jordan; and he became "tetrarch" of Galilee and Perea. Although these two regions were poor, separate geographic areas with few natural resources and no significant cities, Antipas moved quickly to impose Roman-style order. He rebuilt Sepphoris as a modern Roman city called Autocratoris ("belonging to the Emperor") with palace, treasury, forum, and theater, and brought in a new population. This was happening when Jesus was a boy and teenager.

From Autocratoris, the peasant villagers were kept under constant surveillance and tax collection was maximized. When his brother Archelaus was suddenly removed (AD 6), Antipas took the title Herod. After the death of Augustus in AD 14—when Jesus was in his late teens—Antipas announced plans to build a new city headquarters named in honor of the new emperor Tiberius on the shores of Galilee, from where he could control both Galilee and Perea. To the horror of Jews, he built on a cemetery, making its people perpetually *unclean*. This building project further increased the tax burden.

Armies of tax collectors accompanied by soldiers descended on every grove, vineyard, and threshing floor to claim Herod's share—"as much as a third of the total crops and other agricultural products."[2] According to the historian Josephus, Antipas was collecting the equivalent of "about nine tons" of gold annually. If peasant farmers couldn't pay, they were forced to take a loan against the next crop, often from the temple aristocracy, who had money to loan. The peasants' ancestral lands were used as equity.

With new techniques for salting and pickling, fishing on Galilee became an industry, no longer the tranquil work of lone fishermen depicted in illustrated Bibles! Vast quantities of fish were required to meet government quotas, to be taxed and sent to Magdala's processing factories for export to the far reaches of the empire, to bring further wealth into the coffers of Antipas.

Under this regime, village and family culture was torn apart, and the people wondered, *Was this God's punishment for their sins? Would an anointed one ever intervene to redeem and restore their Jewish kingdom?*

John the Baptist's call to "Repent, for the kingdom of heaven is near" (Matthew 3:2) was a direct challenge to Herod Antipas and his aspirations. Seeking to consolidate his claim over all the Jews, Antipas put aside his Nabatean consort to wed a member of the Jewish royal Hasmonean clan.

But in choosing his niece Herodias—the daughter of his half-brother, the Hasmonean prince Aristobulus—he both violated Levitical laws against incest and brazenly took his brother Philip's wife. Herod Antipas was faced with war from his former wife's Nabatean family, and he saw John the Baptist's condemnation of his scheme before the crowds flocking to the Jordan as open revolt. John was thrown into a dungeon on the other side of the Dead Sea.

This was when Jesus returned to Galilee, repeating the Baptist's call to "Repent, for the kingdom of heaven has come near" (Matthew 4:17). He would certainly have been under the constant surveillance of spies from the court of Antipas and Herodias in Tiberias, as well as the wary eye of Jerusalem's Temple authorities.

And then He called a hated tax collector to follow Him!

Levi Matthew became a disciple of Jesus. How might this have undermined Herod Antipas's tax-gathering schemes?

_____

_____

How had Matthew been prepared for Jesus' invitation: "Follow me"? Imagine how the following reports about Jesus had impacted him:

- Jesus' baptism reported by fishermen from Bethsaida (John 1:29-51).

_____

_____

- Jesus' actions in the temple in Jerusalem (John 2:12-25).

_____

_____

- Jesus' healing of the Capernaum official's son—from Cana (John 4:43-54).

_____

_____

- Jesus' message: "Repent, for the kingdom of heaven has come near" (Matthew 4:17).

_____

_____

Review the first six fishing trips: Could these fishing trips have gone unnoticed by Matthew?

_____

_____

What did Matthew do to introduce his friends to Jesus (Luke 5:27-32)?

_____

_____

What accusations were leveled at Jesus, and how did He respond?

_____

_____

How do you understand Jesus' responses to questions about fasting (Matthew 9:14-17)?

_____

_____

What were the implications for Jesus' movement building?

_____

_____

Evaluation: How did Jesus and His disciples do?

Were there nonbelievers present?

_____

_____

How did Jesus present Himself in a culturally relevant way as Messiah and Savior?

_____

_____

Who put their faith in Him or moved closer to accepting Him as Messiah?

_____

_____

SHARING

With your friends:

Who could you invite to a Matthew-type party to meet Jesus?

_____

_____

How, when, and where would you hold such a party?

_____

_____

Spend time praying, and settle on the time and place:

_____

_____

How could your friends who don't yet know Jesus be involved?

_____

_____

GUIDE 21

MORE SABBATH CONTROVERSIES

What Was It This Time?

THE PHARISEES took seriously the role of defining and upholding their social and spiritual boundary markers. "The laws of their Torah, or 'Teachings,' with its legislation for tithes, offerings, Sabbaths, fast days, sabbatical years, and purity standards, enabled the people of Israel to maintain a stable system of social relations, economic welfare and local economy."[1]

But Jesus crossed the boundary in calling a tax collector and then socializing with his friends—money changers, tax collectors, and prostitutes. He further upset the Pharisees by His Sabbath activities and claims. How did these controversies define His movement building? What lessons do we learn for movement building today?

READ
- Matthew 12:1-14; Mark 2:23–3:6; Luke 6:1-11
- *Messiah*, chapter 29

In "Galilee of the Gentiles," where traditional village life was under constant threat from the kingdom-building ambitions of Herod Antipas, the Pharisees were extra diligent in defining the boundaries of Judaism. They imposed numerous regulations on Sabbath-keeping, making it a burden rather than a "delight" (Isaiah 58:13).

Walking with Him in the fields one Sabbath, Jesus' disciples picked and ate grain. How did the Pharisees react (Matthew 12:2; Mark 2:24; Luke 6:2)?

_____

_____

How did Jesus' response confront them?

- Matthew 12:8:

_____

_____

- Mark 2:27-28:

_____

_____

How would they have understood His claims in the light of the Scriptures?

- Genesis 1:1-2; 2:1-3:

_____

_____

- Exodus 20:8-11:

_____

_____

- Deuteronomy 5:12-15:

_____

_____

In their synagogue, Jesus took the initiative, calling a man with a shriveled hand forward and challenging His accusers. "Which is lawful on the Sabbath: to do good or to do evil, to save life or to kill?" he demanded (Mark 3:4). Why do you think He became so angry and distressed (Mark 3:5)?

_____

_____

Jesus' conflict with the Pharisees was clearly escalating. His words—"the Son of Man is Lord even of the Sabbath" (Mark 2:27-28)—and His work of healing left them in no doubt. The Sabbath was the gift of God; healing was the activity of God. Jesus was claiming to be God. In what way was this controversy defining His movement? Explore the following parallels, and suggest other possibilities:

Jesus and Sabbath	Jesus and Kingdom
He is Lord of the Sabbath	He is King—eternal God, Creator God.
It is His day.	It is His kingdom.
It offers "rest" from human effort.	It offers "rest" in Him (Matthew 11:28-30).
It is His work, not ours.	It is His movement, not ours.
Salvation is by His grace.	His movement is one of grace.

What other parallels do you find?

_____

_____

Jesus' movement stood in stark contrast to the conflicting aspiration of both the Pharisees and Herod Antipas, so what drove the Pharisees to "plot with the Herodians how they might kill Jesus" (Mark 3:1-6; also see Matthew 12:9-14; Luke 6:6-11)?

_____

_____

Jesus had taken a major risk. What danger did His movement now face?

_____

_____

SABBATH MIRACLES

Jesus performed seven miracles on Sabbath days. We have explored the first four and will come to the next three in the next phase of Jesus' movement building. Survey each story to identify how Jesus defined Himself and His movement by Sabbath:

• Healing of the invalid at the Pool of Bethesda (John 5:1-18):

_____

_____

- Deliverance from demon possession in Capernaum's synagogue (Luke 4:31-37):

  _____

  _____

- Healing of Peter's mother-in-law that same Sabbath (Luke 4:38-39):

  _____

  _____

- Restoration of a man's shriveled hand (Matthew 12:9-14):

  _____

  _____

- Healing of a crippled woman bound by Satan for eighteen years (Luke 13:10-17):

  _____

  _____

- Healing, in a Pharisee's house, a man with excess body fluid (Luke 14:1-6):

  _____

  _____

- Sight given to a blind man (John 9:1-41):

  _____

  _____

Not one of these miracles was in response to an *accident or emergency* situation! Each person could have waited until the end of the Sabbath, yet Jesus disregarded the rules of the Pharisees and healed them.

REFLECTION

How do you feel about being a follower of Jesus who defined Himself and His movement so courageously?

  _____

  _____

SHARING

With your friends who are sharing this journey with you, discuss what you have discovered about Jesus and His movement of disciplemaking from His passion in these controversial situations.

_____

_____

What qualities of Jesus will you share with your friends who are growing as disciples?

_____

_____

ESSENTIAL FRAMES OF JESUS' MOVEMENT BUILDING

DURING THIS THIRD PHASE, Jesus has been training, equipping, and expanding His outreach. His intentional call for Levi Matthew to join, and the revelation of His identity by His words and works on the Sabbath, were precursors to another transition for Him. In this guide, we review Jesus' journey and take time to reflect, experience, and identify with Him and His movement building.

REVIEW THE JOURNEY

How has your life been changed by walking with Jesus through this phase of equipping for participation in expanded outreach?

_____

_____

What have you come to appreciate about Jesus?

_____

_____

Has the direction of His ministry surprised you? If so, in what ways?

_____

_____

ESSENTIAL FRAMES OF JESUS' *PARTICIPATION AND EQUIPPING* PHASE

Survey guides 15–21 and identify what you believe to be essential frames for Jesus' movement building from this participation and equipping phase.

_____

_____

_____

_____

_____

_____

_____

_____

_____

Review essential frames from the preparation phase of Jesus' life (Phase 1):

- The person: Jesus
- The principle: status reversal
- The purpose: to do the Father's will
- The *person of peace*: key in relational streams

Review essential frames from the ministry foundation phase (Phase 2):

- Jesus' five invitations.
- Jesus' reliance on Holy Spirit POWER.
- Jesus' movement encompassed all people.
- Jesus' message is His method—a journey of descent for us.
- Jesus is the temple.

What other priorities have you identified from phases 1 and 2?

_____

_____

REFLECTION

What has surprised you in how Jesus modeled and equipped His disciples to participate in His movement?

_____

_____

While the Samaritan woman responded quickly, Matthew took time before accepting Jesus' invitation. Both were equipped to share their testimonies and invite others to Jesus. What fresh ideas did you get from how they did this (John 4:1-42; Luke 5:27-32)?

_____

_____

How are the invitations of Jesus to "Come and see," "Follow me," and "Fish with me" impacting your life?

_____

_____

To what extent have you incorporated Jesus' movement-building approach into your life?

_____

_____

SHARING

What will you share with your friends who are on this journey with you?

_____

_____

In what way has this participation and equipping phase impacted you?

_____

_____

How has God convicted you—and for what purpose?

_____

_____

In what way is your life being changed by Jesus' priorities?

_____

_____

As a result of exploring the first three phases of Jesus' life and disciplemaking, how are you now relating to those you are encouraging to know and follow Jesus as disciples?

_____

_____

Leadership Multiplication
MOVEMENT THROUGH SACRIFICIAL LOVE

MUCH DISCIPLEMAKING HAS involved believing, behaving, and then belonging. However, Jesus cultivated a process of four concentric responses to His invitations:

1. Belonging	"Come and see"	Experiential
2. Behaving	"Follow me"	Relational
3. Believing	"Fish with me"	Participatory
4. Being	"Love your enemies"	Sacrificial

Sometimes little heed is given to this fourth dimension: the transformation of being or worldview. This is of critical concern, because the control center for life is worldview[1] and, if this is unchallenged, we will continue to operate out of ego and the desire for status. The Gospel writers provide a corrective, dedicating most of their records to how Jesus modeled a worldview shaped by the value of care for others. Supreme self-denial and sacrifice motivated by loving concern for others might be called a *cruciform worldview*.[2]

During this fourth phase of movement building, Jesus multiplies leaders, but it is not merely a matter of numbers. He works tirelessly to transform their worldview. His Kingdom movement is founded on sacrificial love, even for enemies. This phase is challenging and confronting. It begins with a night of prayer and the selection of twelve apostles from among His disciples and culminates in Jesus' arrival in Bethany for His final Passover in Jerusalem.

At the appointment of the twelve apostles, Jesus introduced His fourth

invitation. It was countercultural and counterintuitive: "Love your enemies" (Matthew 5:44). It is an invitation to deny self and sacrifice for
others, to identify with God's nature. Transformation of worldview was a
priority for Him. And, during this phase of *leadership multiplication*, Jesus
intensified His movement-building activities and teaching.

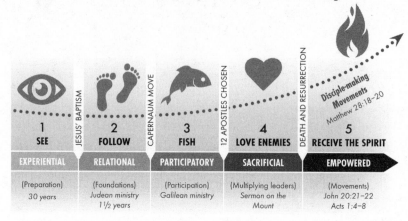

This phase covers sections 53–127 in *The NIV Harmony of the Gospels*
and chapters 30–61 in *Messiah*.

A NIGHT IN PRAYER

Choosing Leaders

IT WAS AN EXCITING but dangerous time for Jesus. Levi Matthew's decision to join His movement undermined the tax-gathering schemes of Herod Antipas, and Jesus' Sabbath activities displayed little regard for Pharisee-imposed national boundary markers. They were angered by His claim to be "Lord of the Sabbath" and the large crowds from Judea, Jerusalem, Idumea, Decapolis, Perea, and Phoenicia that followed Him through Galilee (Mark 3:8). Those Jesus healed knew He was anointed by the Spirit to "proclaim justice to the nations" (Matthew 12:18) and evil spirits "fell down before him," declaring "'You are the Son of God'" (Mark 3:11).

Jesus undermined the spiritual authority of the Pharisees, and His popularity posed a political threat to Antipas. While He had no nationalistic aspirations, these men were not to be messed with! The Pharisees and Herodians—Herod's soldiers or a supportive political party[1]—were plotting "how they might kill Jesus" (Matthew 12:14; Mark 3:6).

It was time for prayer, to seek His Father's counsel, and to multiply leadership to ensure His movement continued. Jesus went to an isolated mountainside, calling just "those he wanted" to meet Him there (Mark 3:13).

READ
- Mark 3:13-19; Luke 6:12-16
- *Messiah*, chapter 30

Why a night in prayer? Try to imagine how His conversation with His Father went.

What do you think Jesus talked with His Father about?

_____

_____

CHOOSING LEADERS
Why did Jesus select the twelve He chose?

_____

_____

Here are key principles for choosing leaders for movements:

- *Prayer.* Jesus was dependent on His Father for leadership selection. What are the implications for us of His night in prayer?

  _____

  _____

- *Experience.* Where did Jesus look for leaders? What could this mean for us (Luke 6:12-16)?

  _____

  _____

- *Introduced.* Why do you think it was important that Jesus affirmed His chosen leaders publicly? What would this have meant to the twelve, His other disciples, and the crowds?

  _____

  _____

- *Purpose.* Jesus called them *apostles* to describe their purpose. What three reasons did He have for choosing them as leaders? What do these reasons mean for you (Mark 3:14-15)?

  _____

  _____

  _____

- *Symbolism.* In the early church, others—both men and women—were chosen as apostles, but the Twelve were His first leadership team.

_____

_____

What do we know about the twelve Jesus chose?

_____

_____

In what ways was Jesus' choice of twelve an undisguised declaration to temple authorities and Antipas that His was a Kingdom movement?

_____

_____

Examine the unusual composition of Jesus' leadership team. In what ways did His selection represent a worldview of status reversal and love for enemies?

_____

_____

A CLOSER LOOK

The twelve apostles have been called a "dirty dozen."[2] What character attributes was Jesus looking for? What are the implications for us?

_____

_____

Levi Matthew, a hated tax collector, was a relatively new disciple. Why was he included?

_____

_____

Was His selection of Judas a miscalculation on Jesus' part? What can we learn from His inclusion?

_____

_____

Many movements fail because of a lack of adaptive methods and structures.[3] Survey the phases of Jesus' movement so far, and identify the basic structures or approaches used:

- *Preparation phase:*

    (For example, learning from others and listening to His Father.)

    _____

    _____

- *Foundation phase:*

    (For example, personal interviews and dialogue, identifying persons of peace.)

    _____

    _____

- *Participation phase:*

    (For example, selecting specific people to equip by modeling and releasing.)

    _____

    _____

- *Leadership multiplication:*

    (For example, investing fully in a team of leaders, challenging their worldviews, and equipping them to multiply.)

    _____

    _____

SHARING

What will you share with your team from how Jesus chose leaders from His disciples?

_____

_____

What could you share with those you are encouraging to know Jesus better?

_____

_____

JESUS' UPSIDE-DOWN GAME PLAN

Invitation Four

IN THE FACE of the growing threat of imprisonment or execution, Jesus multiplied leaders for His movement. Having selected the twelve apostles, He came down the mountainside with them to a level place where a "large crowd of his disciples" and a "great number of people" had gathered.

The atmosphere was electric. The people "had come to hear him and to be healed of their diseases." People were clamoring to touch Him "because power was coming from him and healing them all" (Luke 6:17-19). In this setting, Jesus looked at His large crowd of disciples and shared His countercultural game plan.[1]

Compared to the Greco-Roman thinking and Jewish national hopes, the worldview Jesus shared in His "Sermon on the Mount" was *upside down*. It reflects a radically different picture of God—One of love, the God of *the other*!

READ
  • Matthew 5:1–7:29; Luke 6:17-49
  • *Messiah*, chapter 31

We will survey what Jesus said, identifying the core value of Jesus' worldview and the Kingdom movement that He was cultivating.

KINGDOM PEOPLE (MATTHEW 5:1-16; LUKE 6:20-26)

Jesus and His disciples were surrounded with broken people. Village family life was being eroded, they were suffering violent oppression, loved ones had been snatched away, land was taken in lieu of excessive taxes, and it was a struggle to feed themselves.

Who did Jesus affirm as blessed?[2]

_____

_____

Why might we consider these the wrong people to build a movement on?

_____

_____

What was Jesus teaching His newly designated leaders?

_____

_____

KINGDOM LIVING (MATTHEW 5:17-48; LUKE 6:27-36)

Jesus contrasted Pharisaical morality with God's character. He first confronted any attempt to minimize or dodge around what He was saying (Matthew 5:17-19), then addressed six familiar life situations.

What significance do you find in the statements of Jesus that frame this discussion?

- Matthew 5:20:

_____

_____

- Matthew 5:48:

_____

_____

Jesus introduced each life situation with the words: "You have heard that it was said . . ." then drew the contrast with "But I tell you . . ." Jesus addressed murder, adultery, divorce, honesty, retaliation, and enemies. He was drawing a contrast, not between the Ten Commandments and Himself but between Himself and the views of the Pharisees.[3]

When Jesus quoted Scripture, what phrase did He always use (Matthew 4:4, 6, 10)?

_____

_____

How countercultural was Jesus' idea of Kingdom life?

_____

_____

Pharisees meticulously guarded their prescriptions of Jewish law. In what ways do you think Jesus' contrasts placed them against the crowds on the hillside? How liberating would Jesus' worldview have been?

- For women:

  _____

- For slaves (which was most of them):

  _____

  _____

- For the oppressed:

  _____

  _____

- For others:

  _____

  _____

Soldiers ruthlessly ensured allegiance to Rome and Herod Antipas. How do you think the crowds and soldiers related to Jesus' plan of nonviolent but noncooperative responses to humiliating aggression by "an evil person" (Matthew 5:38-42)?

_____

_____

"If someone strikes you on the right cheek, turn to him the other also": The backhanded blow was that of superiors—masters to slaves, husbands to wives, Romans to Jews—to insult and humiliate. Turning the left cheek disarmed the assailant, leaving slapping or punching the only option, for culturally the left hand could not be used—*only people of equal status fought that way!*[4]

"If someone wants to sue you and take your tunic, let him have your cloak as well": Many of the poor only had one or two garments. Stripped of their houses, lands, and even their outer garments by oppressive taxes and debts, Jesus advised them to hand over their underwear as well. Already robbed of dignity, walking naked in the street would shame their oppressors—*turning the tables!*[5]

"If [a soldier] forces you to [carry his pack] one mile, go with him two miles": A Roman soldier could demand a Jew to carry his equipment, but only for a mile. Those subjected to such indignity would have seen the twist in the generosity Jesus advocated. A soldier would be left pleading for his pack to be put down to avoid tough discipline by his commanding officer.[6]

Can you suggest other creative, strong, and nonviolent responses to evil?

_____

_____

INVITATION FOUR: "LOVE YOUR ENEMIES"

Jesus reminded the crowds of the accepted teaching—and drew a sharp contrast:

> You have heard that it was said, "Love your neighbor and hate your enemy." But I tell you: "Love your enemies and pray for those who persecute you, that you may be [true children][7] of your Father in heaven."
>
> MATTHEW 5:43-45

How counterintuitive and countercultural is this worldview
(Matthew 5:43-48; Luke 6:32-36)?

_____

_____

How do we love those we don't like? How do we become more loving?

_____

_____

JESUS' GAME PLAN

Jesus was moving to establish His Kingdom. The crowds were restless, the Pharisees incensed, the soldiers watching for rebellion, and the disciples waiting to implement a plan to liberate Israel. When He shared the strategy, it must have sounded crazy, and it still does: *"Love your enemies—for this is God's attitude"* (Matthew 5:44, author's paraphrase).

How do you think they each responded to such a radical, crazy game plan?[8]

_____

_____

Such radical, countercultural love re-orders a person's motives, priorities, and relationships.

What is the motivation for your religious activities (Matthew 6:1-18)?

_____

_____

Jesus was speaking to desperate people, struggling to survive with the necessities of life—money, housing, clothes, and food. How do you relate to Jesus' priorities (Matthew 6:19-33)?

_____

_____

Speaking to people who had suffered the worst abuse, Jesus said, "Stop judging and condemning—and forgive" (author's paraphrase). How will you apply His radical plan to your relationships (Matthew 7:1-29; Luke 6:37-49)?

_____

_____

Jesus' worldview and game plan were radical. It must have shocked and disappointed His disciples, yet they were to lead. As Jesus said, "The blind cannot lead the blind; and students cannot be above their teacher!" (Luke 6:39-40, author's paraphrase). Perhaps Jesus sensed unease, saying: "Why do you call me, 'Lord, Lord,' and do not do what I say?" (Luke 6:46). From this time on, Jesus worked tirelessly to transform their worldview, for His Kingdom movement is founded on sacrificial love, even for enemies.

REFLECTION

What have you discovered in the teachings of Jesus in this guide that you were not familiar with?

SHARING

How will you now treat those who have insulted and falsely said evil against you?

How will you share the core value of Jesus' worldview with those you are leading to Him?

LEADERSHIP AND AUTHORITY

JESUS MOVED to multiply leadership. Following a night in prayer with His Father, He selected twelve disciples, designated them as apostles, and then confronted them, His other disciples, and the crowd with His upside-down worldview and His Kingdom game plan. Spend a few moments reviewing the core of what He said in Matthew 5:43-48:

What was His worldview?

_____

_____

What was His game plan?

_____

_____

What do you know about the twelve Jesus chose as apostles, His leadership team? Who would have been highly suspicious of the others? Who were enemies? In what way did they represent a microcosm of His Kingdom worldview of loving their enemies?

_____

_____

READ

- Matthew 7:28–8:13; Luke 7:1-17
- *Messiah*, chapter 32

What was the reaction of the crowds to Jesus' Sermon on the Mount (Matthew 7:28–8:1)?

_____

_____

What gave authority to Jesus' teachings?

_____

_____

TWO KINDS OF AUTHORITY CONTRASTED

Jesus multiplied leaders for His growing movement, to multiply Himself. His teaching *authority* was recognized. This authority was not coercive; He did not impose His will on anyone. It was intrinsic authority; it came from within. People recognized that He spoke like no other man. His word was compelling and authoritative.

When He descended from the mountain to Capernaum, He received a request on behalf of a Roman centurion—one "under *authority*" or under the command of another (Luke 7:1-8). This provided an opportunity for Jesus to share some lessons with His apostles.

What do we learn about this Roman centurion and how he handled the kind of authority he knew in the army?

_____

_____

How did the centurion's authority contrast with Jesus' radical love for His enemies?

_____

_____

But what amazed Jesus about this man?

_____

_____

Reflect on the two kinds of authority contrasted in this story:

Centurion's authority	Jesus' authority

Mark Edwards observes that "love, humility, faith and authority are all principles of godly leadership."[1] Jesus modeled these qualities. Were they at all evident in the centurion's exercise of authority? And how are these qualities evident in your leadership?

Soon after, Jesus visited Nain, a village nine miles south of Nazareth. As He approached the town gate, a funeral procession was leaving, with men carrying the body of a widow's only son. Jesus demonstrated His authority over death, raising the boy to life and returning him to his mother (Luke 7:11-17).

AUTHORITY AND HUMILITY

Read: Philippians 2:1-11

In what way does Paul's master story reflect Jesus' worldview?

How does this relate to leadership and authority?

REFLECTION

What was new for you in this guide?

Think of a situation in which you are a leader—home, work, among friends, church, small group, in your community. What principles of leadership authority will you apply?

_____

_____

SHARING

What have you learned about authority and being a leader that you will share with friends?

_____

_____

For those you are leading to Jesus, what have you found in these stories that will be appealing?

_____

_____

LEADERSHIP AND DOUBT

JOHN THE BAPTIST was in prison. His voice had been silenced; his ministry ended. This would have been particularly difficult for him, as he was accustomed to living in the wilderness, an activist on a popular mission attracting huge attention. With confidence, he had proclaimed Jesus to be "the one" to come, "the Lamb of God, who takes away the sin of the world" and "the Son of God" (John 1:26-29, 34-36). Now from his dungeon he sends two of his disciples to ask his cousin Jesus, "Are you the one who was to come, or should we expect someone else?" (Matthew 11:3; Luke 7:19).

John was beginning to doubt his own message. He had given his life to proclaim Jesus was the long-awaited Messiah, but he was now in danger of *falling away* (Matthew 11:6; Luke 7:23). Why the doubt? How quickly do we doubt? What is the impact of doubt? In this story, we learn from Jesus about leadership and doubt.

READ
- Matthew 11:2-30; Luke 7:18-35
- *Messiah*, chapter 34

John's disciples reported all Jesus was doing. Why was this unsettling John?

_____

_____

When John's disciples came to Jesus, He was surrounded by crowds who had come for healing and deliverance. Try to imagine their faces when they heard of John's doubts—remembering that he had pointed many of them to Jesus, including some of the Twelve.[1]

What was Jesus' response? What messages were John's disciples to take back?

_____

_____

- Report:

  _____

  _____

- Scripture: Jesus quoted two Scriptures for His cousin, including verses shared in the synagogue in Nazareth when He was rejected by His townspeople (Isaiah 35:5-6, 61:1; compare Luke 4:17-19). Why might these prophecies have reassured John?

  _____

  _____

- Encouragement (Matthew 11:6; Luke 7:23):

  _____

  _____

As John's disciples were leaving, Jesus spoke with the crowd about John. It is possible they heard some of what He said. Again, He quoted the Word of God.

Why had they gone out to see John (compare Isaiah 40:1-5)?

_____

_____

In what way was John "more than a prophet" (compare Malachi 3:1)?

_____

_____

Jesus said, "He is the Elijah who was to come" (Matthew 11:14; compare Malachi 4:5-6), and "no one greater" has been born, "yet the one who is least in the kingdom of God is greater than he" (Luke 7:28). What do you think Jesus meant?

_____

_____

How had both John and Jesus been misunderstood (Matthew 11:16-19; Luke 7:29-35)?

_____

_____

In what way do you think Jesus' outburst, prayer, and invitation might have also been for his cousin's benefit (Matthew 11:20-30)?

_____

_____

MORE ABOUT JOHN
Compare these Scriptures that refer to John the Baptist as Elijah:

- Malachi 4:5-6:

  _____

  _____

- Luke 1:5-17:

  _____

  _____

Also look at Scriptures that speak of John preparing the way for Jesus:

- Isaiah 40:1-5:

  _____

  _____

- Luke 1:57-80:

  _____

  _____

- Luke 3:1-23; compare Mark 1:1-8:

  _____

  _____

And another reference to John as Elijah:

- Matthew 17:1-13:

_____

_____

REFLECTIONS

What can cause doubts in leaders?

_____

_____

How real was the risk of John the Baptist falling away?

_____

_____

What could have been the ramifications if he had fallen away?

_____

_____

How long does it take you to go from belief to doubt?

_____

_____

How do you handle misunderstanding and doubt?

_____

_____

How might doubt be beneficial?

_____

_____

How are you known? Do sinners call you a friend (Matthew 11:19; Luke 7:34)?

_____

_____

SHARING

What will you share with your friends this week from your study and reflections?

_____

_____

What can you share with those you are leading to Jesus?

_____

_____

LEADERSHIP AND GRATITUDE

JESUS WAS TEACHING the twelve apostles about leadership. He defined His worldview, then explored *authority* and *doubt*. In honoring His cousin John, Jesus drew a contrast between the accusations against John the Baptist—he "came neither eating nor drinking, and they say, 'He has a demon'"—and Himself—"Here is a glutton and a drunkard, a friend of tax collectors and sinners" (Matthew 11:18-19). An invitation to have dinner with a Pharisee provided the perfect opportunity to illustrate how to handle offense as leaders, as well as speak of *gratitude, forgiveness,* and *salvation.*

This is a disturbing story. Pharisees were plotting with the Herodians how to get rid of Jesus (Mark 3:6; compare Matthew 12:14; Luke 6:11), but, at this stage, their schemes were hidden, their contempt veiled. With His reputation growing among the common people, Jesus posed a threat to "the orthodox guardians of the faith." A dinner discussion gave opportunity to "humiliate and embarrass him."[1]

READ
* Luke 7:36-50

Pharisees defined their holiness "through an arduous allegiance to ritual purity rules,"[2] and meals gave opportunity to demonstrate this. Inviting Jesus—a teacher of growing popularity—to his home afforded Simon such an opportunity. What do you learn about Simon from this story?[3]

_____

_____

Simon's plan to humiliate Jesus unraveled when Jesus accepted the touch of an uninvited woman. What do we know about this woman? What brought her to Simon's home? Why this extraordinary and embarrassing display of emotion?

_____

_____

Many women delivered from difficult experiences accompanied Jesus and the twelve apostles in their travels (Luke 8:1-3). What impression might they have made on this woman? Do you think she might have become one of them?

_____

_____

It seems Simon didn't realize where Jesus' story was leading. In what way was the woman's response a calculated rebuke of Simon's intolerable treatment of all those he considered unacceptable to God (including Jesus)?

_____

_____

THROUGH MIDDLE EASTERN EYES

It is helpful to read this story with an understanding of the culture of the time.[4] For such banquets, the gates and doors were open to all, but there were protocols. Guests were welcomed with great fanfare—a kiss from the host, their shoes removed—then guided to their place of status on a couch or a small stool around a long, low U-shaped table where "water and olive oil would be brought for . . . washing of hands and feet." Olive oil was used like soap.[5]

In the center of the room, large wooden food bowls would have been arranged along the low table, as well as on the floor. There might also have been stone serving trays, plates, bowls, and cups, some beautifully decorated. It is possible there was also glassware from the glass factories of Jerusalem. Such vessels could not become ritually unclean like porous pottery, an important consideration for a pious Pharisee.[6]

Hovering in the background behind the slaves and servants, the uninvited from the community gathered to observe and "eavesdrop on the conversation." This was accepted custom, providing the Pharisee further opportunities to demonstrate his holiness.

With this context, we observe:

Jesus was invited but not welcomed. He was snubbed: not welcomed with a kiss, water for his feet, or oil. Michael Frost observes: "For a host to omit any detail of this ritual would have been unthinkable and a gross insult to the guest."[7]

Jesus entered the home and "reclined at the table." This was unexpected. In a shame–honor culture, He might have exploded in rage and stormed out, shaming His host; or having been snubbed as He was, He could have endured the insult in silence, refusing any future contact. But what he did was more dramatic. The eldest in the room was expected to recline first.[8] Only a little older than thirty, it is unlikely Jesus was the oldest present, but having been treated in the most despicable, offensive manner, He reclined on the couch as if He were the eldest and most highly honored in the room!

A woman "who had lived a sinful life in that town" came uninvited (Luke 7:37). This could be expected, but her emotional display was not! Having endured scorn and humiliation, she understood Simon's rebuff of Jesus was calculated to humiliate, mock, and embarrass Him. As a recipient of salvation and forgiveness, she identified with Simon's humiliated guest—her suffering Savior!

GRATITUDE FOR FORGIVENESS AND SALVATION

Did the woman come to be forgiven or because she was forgiven?

Jesus indicated that she had observed His humiliation by Simon (Luke 7:45). In contrast, and no doubt offended by Simon's disdain, she recognized Jesus as her Messiah and Savior, believing that "her many sins have been forgiven" (Luke 7:47). How did she express her gratitude (Luke 7:38)?

Reflect on this woman's identification with Jesus and His suffering:

- She wept uncontrollably, washing Jesus' feet with her tears of gratitude.
- She wiped Jesus' feet with her hair, which was embarrassing and improper, for women only uncovered their hair in the presence of their husbands—and then rarely!
- She kissed Jesus' feet and bathed them in perfume, maybe a symbol of her past impurity and vain attempts to smother the shame of her life with sweaty men.

Imagine Simon's embarrassment as the tables turned:[9]

- Like the prostitute, he was in debt to God.
- Like the prostitute, he could not repay the debt.
- Like the prostitute, God had canceled his debt.

Why was he not as excited and thankful as the forgiven woman?

_____

_____

Traditional taboos no longer mattered to this woman. She was forgiven and in the presence of her Savior. What was Jesus modeling in letting her carry on, welcoming and drawing attention to her as a positive example of gratitude? What was His attitude toward traditional taboos about women (Luke 7:48-50)?

REFLECTION

From this experience, what insights into movement building might the twelve apostles have learned for their leadership roles?

_____

_____

Self-righteousness is a grave evil. It makes us smug. It blinds us to reality. It robs us of joy. It makes us proud and critical of others. It makes us judgmental.

Forgiveness and salvation are displayed in gratitude. Those who carry the greatest debt love their Savior the most! The most grateful tell their stories with the most passion and emotion! Gratitude transforms their lives.

Although it might be counterintuitive, who could contribute most effectively to your movement development?

_____

_____

SHARING
What will you share with your friends this week?

_____

_____

What can you share with those you are leading to Jesus?

_____

_____

LEADERSHIP AND REJECTION

INSULT AND REJECTION can be the lot of Christian leaders. Unfortunately, some bring reproach on themselves and the character of Jesus by their arrogance, manipulation, politics, discrimination, and shameful abuse. But with Jesus, it was His ministry of healing and deliverance—His profound goodness—that brought derision.

Don't expect faithfulness to God's agenda to always be rewarded with accolades. Attacks can come from the most unexpected sources—even from within the church! In this guide, we look at how Jesus handled His first public rejection by Jewish leaders.

READ

- Luke 8:1-3; Matthew 12:22-50; Mark 3:20-35; Luke 8:19-21
- *Messiah*, chapter 33

First, we read of Jesus traveling with the twelve apostles and some women who were supporting His ministry financially. What do we learn about these women (Luke 8:1-3)?

REJECTED AS DEMONIC

In contrast to the gratitude and support of the women, how did the Pharisees react to Jesus healing a demon-possessed, blind, and mute man (Matthew 12:22-37; Mark 3:20-30)?

_____

_____

Why did Jesus label their accusations blasphemous?

_____

_____

Why do you think attributing the Holy Spirit's activity to Beelzebub was "unpardonable"?

_____

_____

Jesus was performing miracles. Why do you think He responded so pointedly to requests for "a miraculous sign" (Matthew 12:38-45)?

_____

_____

What was the significance of the sign they would receive?

_____

_____

What leadership lessons do you find in Jesus' response to His detractors?

_____

_____

WOES AND WARNINGS

There were also other occasions when Jesus was accused of doing miracles by demonic power.

Read: Matthew 9:18-34; Luke 11:14–13:9

The second followed three miracles of healing (Matthew 9:18-34): "The crowd was amazed and said, 'Nothing like this has ever been seen in Israel.' But the Pharisees said, 'It is by the prince of demons that he drives out demons'" (Matthew 9:33-34).

The third also followed a dramatic healing—the deliverance of a demon-possessed mute. Again, some "tested" Jesus "by asking for a sign from heaven" (Luke 11:14-16).

Each blasphemous accusation provided Jesus with major teaching opportunities.

Do not miss this statement: "Blessed . . . are those who hear the word of God and obey it" (Luke 11:28). Keep this in mind as you reflect on Jesus' feisty confrontation at a Pharisee's meal table.

Woes to Pharisees (Luke 11:37-54):
What were the issues?

_____

_____

Why do you think Jesus was prepared to "insult" these "experts in the law"?

_____

_____

Warnings for disciples (Luke 12:1-59):
How do you think the twelve apostles reacted to Jesus' teaching? And what application will you make in your life and leadership to address His warnings?

_____

_____

- Hypocrisy (Luke 12:1-12):

_____

_____

- Greed and wealth (Luke 12:13-34):

_____

_____

- Being unprepared for the Son of Man's coming (Luke 12:35-48):

_____

_____

- Coming divisions (Luke 12:49-53):

_____

_____

- Failure to discern the times (Luke 12:54-59):

_____

_____

Repent or perish (Luke 13:1-9):

What was Jesus' point for His listeners—and for you?

_____

_____

HANDLING REJECTION

Fear of rejection can paralyze a disciple's witness. What encouragement have you found in Jesus' experiences and teaching?

_____

_____

How might God use rejection as an opportunity to transform our lives?

_____

_____

Where did Jesus find kinship and support, and where will you find yours (Matthew 12:46-50; Mark 3:31-35; Luke 8:19-21; compare Mark 3:13-15)?

_____

_____

SHARING

What will you share with your friends this week?

_____

_____

What can you share with those you are leading to Jesus?

_____

_____

LEADERSHIP AND MOVEMENT FOUNDATIONS

"THAT SAME DAY Jesus went out of the house and sat by the lake" (Matthew 13:1). It had already been a full and exhausting day—delivering a demon-possessed man who was both blind and mute, facing accusations of blasphemy, responding to the Pharisees' cynical demands for "a miraculous sign," and engaging with His family. But there were large crowds to teach, and the time was ripe to outline the foundational principles of His Kingdom movement with His twelve apostles.

His movement stood in stark contrast to the religious and political aspirations of those plotting His demise—the Pharisees and Herodians. His teaching method reflected His message: using parables from everyday life that people could understand. Jesus first taught the crowds by the sea, then He went into a house, where His disciples joined Him for further explanations—and more parables.

READ
- Matthew 13:1-53; Mark 4:1-34; Luke 8:4-18

What did Jesus want the people to understand from His parables about farmers, markets, and fishermen?

_____

_____

What have you discovered about the nature of God's Kingdom from:

- The different soils?

_____

_____

Good soil has been worked and turned over, and is full of nutrients, perhaps compost and manure. What might this say about the most receptive—those who produce a multiplying crop?

_____

_____

- The seed's spontaneous growth?

_____

_____

- The good seed and weeds?

_____

_____

- The mustard seed?

_____

_____

A mustard tree can grow to a height of twenty to twenty-three feet. What point do you think Jesus was making with this parable?

_____

_____

- The leavened bread?

_____

_____

Jesus spoke of the small amount of yeast needed to leaven a large loaf. What does this say about people and the Kingdom?

_____

_____

- The hidden treasure and the pearl?

_____

_____

- The fishing net?

_____

_____

THE FOUR FIELDS: MOVEMENT FOUNDATIONS (MARK 4:26-29)

The Kingdom parables disclose "the secret of the kingdom of God" (Mark 4:11). Jesus' short parable of a farmer sowing seed and its spontaneous growth to produce a harvest is today inspiring movements of multiplying new churches:[1]

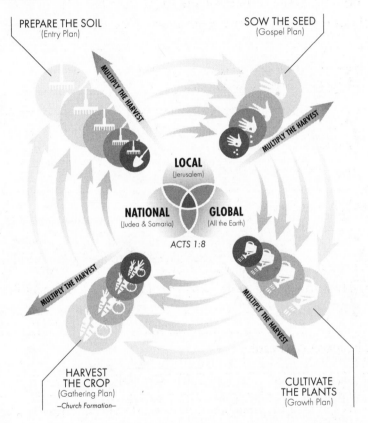

Identify an empty field—a community, people group, or the homes of family or friends who need to know Jesus. What do you identify as key movement issues?

_____

_____

How could you prepare and enter an empty field?

_____

_____

What might you sow, and how will you do this, so that the seed grows "all by itself"?

_____

_____

How could you cooperate with God's work to cultivate the growth of disciples?

_____

_____

What shape might the gathering or harvest take?

_____

_____

And how could this multiply?

_____

_____

Farmers in the Middle East harvest for seed to sow into the fields in the next season. They keep the best seed for multiplication. They "sow in tears," going out "weeping" for their families are hungry; but unless they plant, they will starve (Psalm 126:5-6).

Why is the multiplication of new disciples, with new groups and churches, so important?

- It puts us in tune with God's missionary heart.
- It places us where the Holy Spirit is at work outside church.
- It is the way to hand faith on to next generations.
- It engages with where the future church is!
- It puts us in touch with our New Testament and faith heritage.

REFLECTION

What has stood out to you in this section?

_____

_____

SHARING

What will you share with your friends this week?

_____

_____

Do you have friends who are growing as followers of Jesus, who could gather as a new group or church to explore their journey with God together?

_____

_____

What can you share with those you are leading to Jesus?

_____

_____

GUIDE 30

LEADERSHIP AND
TOUGH ASSIGNMENTS

MOVEMENT LEADERS do not shirk tough mission assignments. They are not sitting in administrative offices directing others to make disciples. They are on the front line, multiplying disciples and other movement leaders. Jesus modeled this to His twelve apostles.

It takes courage to make the moves that advance a movement. Physically and emotionally exhausted—with little time for meals, family, or rest—Jesus "gave orders to cross to the other side of the lake" (Matthew 8:18). It was time for retreat—and advance. The toughest experiences were ahead: physical danger, demon possession, long-term suffering, a child's death, blasphemous accusations, and rejection by His own. How did He handle these? What were the limits to what He could accomplish? What do we learn?

READ
- Matthew 8:18, 23-34, 9:18-34, 13:54-58; Mark 4:35–5:43, 6:1-6; Luke 8:22-56
- *Messiah*, chapters 35–36

Physical danger: in a deadly storm (Matthew 8:18, 23-27; Mark 4:35-41; Luke 8:22-25)

What were key issues in this experience?

_____

_____

Why was this experience important for the Twelve?

_____

_____

What life lessons were they to learn from this experience?

_____

_____

Demon possession: at Gadara (Matthew 8:28-34; Mark 5:1-20; Luke 8:26-39)

What were key issues in this experience?

_____

_____

Why was this experience important for the Twelve?

_____

_____

What life lessons were they to learn from this experience?

_____

_____

Death of a child: a desperate father (Matthew 9:18-26; Mark 5:21-43; Luke 8:40-56)

What were key issues in this experience?

_____

_____

Why was this experience important for the Twelve?

_____

_____

What life lessons were they to learn from this experience?

_____

_____

Long-term suffering: despair and faith (Matthew 9:20-22; Mark 5:24-34; Luke 8:42-48)

What were key issues in this experience?

_____

_____

Why was this experience important for the Twelve?

_____

_____

What life lessons were they to learn from this experience?

_____

_____

False accusations: blasphemy (Matthew 9:27-34)

What were key issues in this experience?

_____

_____

Why was this experience important for the Twelve?

_____

_____

What life lessons were they to learn from this experience?

_____

_____

Rejection: by His own (Matthew 13:54-58; Mark 6:1-6)

What were key issues in this experience?

_____

_____

Why was this experience important for the Twelve?

_____

_____

What life lessons were they to learn from this experience?

_____

_____

Of all the experiences above, which would you find most confronting?

_____

_____

What encouragement have you received for your most difficult mission assignments?

_____

_____

CROSSING TO "THE OTHER SIDE": INSIGHTS FOR MOVEMENT LEADERS

Going "to the other side" (Matthew 8:18; Mark 4:35; Luke 8:22) was a major change of focus for Jesus and His disciples, for those on the eastern shores of the lake were Gentile-pagans, not predominantly Jews.

How might Jesus' disciples (all Jews) have felt about going "to the other side"?

_____

_____

What was Jesus teaching about movement leadership?

_____

_____

With little time for meals, family, or rest, how could going "to the other side" bring you refreshment as well as new opportunities for movement building?

_____

_____

What storms are threatening to overwhelm you—at home, work, or elsewhere? Are you ready to cry out, "Lord, save us!" (Matthew 8:25)?

_____

_____

"You of little faith, why are you so afraid?" Jesus asked (Matthew 8:26). Mark Edwards comments: "He didn't expect them to still the storm. He just expected them to know Him well enough by now to know that He was never too busy or too tired to save the day."[1] How does this redefine faith?

_____

_____

The demoniac was a person of peace. Jesus sent him back into his relational stream: "Go home to your family and tell them how much the Lord has done for you" (Mark 5:19). What do you learn from this story for movement building (Mark 5:18-20; Luke 8:38-39)?

_____

_____

REFLECTION

What has been the most helpful insight in this guide for you?

_____

_____

SHARING

What will you share with your friends this week?

_____

_____

What can you share with those you are leading to Jesus?

_____

_____

LEADERSHIP IN TIMES OF CRISIS

JESUS WAS ON THE MOVE, visiting "all the towns and villages" in Galilee. He was "teaching in their synagogues, preaching the good news of the kingdom and healing every disease and sickness" (Matthew 9:35). According to Josephus, there were 204 towns and villages in this predominantly Jewish territory on the western shores of the lake, which extended towards Tyre and Sidon on the Mediterranean. To the north in Gaulanitis (Golan) and east of the Sea of Galilee in Decapolis, the towns were mainly pagan.[1]

The movement was attracting crowds, but there was a shortage of workers, Herod Antipas was upset, and Jesus was grieving John the Baptist's brutal death. Such crises can distract and overwhelm. What can we learn from how Jesus as disciplemaker and movement leader handled these dangerous times?

READ
- Matthew 9:35–11:1, 14:1-12; Mark 6:6-30; Luke 9:1-10
- *Messiah*, chapters 37–38

What part do you think Jesus' intense activity played in growing His movement?

_____

_____

What was the burden of Jesus' heart (Matthew 9:35-38)?

_____

_____

SHORTAGE OF WORKERS

How did Jesus address the shortage of workers (Matthew 10:1-42)?

_____

_____

Imagine being one of the twelve apostles sent out. What would have been on your mind?

_____

_____

What key insights do you take from Jesus' instructions?

_____

_____

Why leave behind extra material comforts?

_____

_____

What is the significance of searching for a certain kind of person?

_____

_____

What lessons do you think the Twelve gained from this mission venture?

_____

_____

DANGEROUS TIMES

John the Baptist attracted a lot of attention. The Jewish people were expecting a messiah. While it didn't mention Jesus or John the Baptist, the Dead Sea Scrolls Manuscript 4Q246—from about a century earlier—reflected this expectation:

Affliction will come on Earth. . . . He will be called great. . . . "Son of God" he will be called and the "Son of the Most High" they will call him. His kingdom will be an everlasting kingdom. . . . He will judge the earth in truth and all will make peace.[2]

John the Baptist believed his mission had been prophesied, quoting from Isaiah 40:3: "a voice of one calling in the desert, 'Prepare the way for the Lord, make straight paths for him'" (Matthew 3:3).

Even Herod Antipas "liked to listen to him" (Mark 6:20). However, John had rebuked Antipas for his marriage to Herodias, his brother Philip's wife (Mark 6:18-19). Herodias was angry, John was imprisoned, and Antipas' birthday celebrations gave opportunity for her to trap her husband—in front of his high officials and military commanders—into delivering to her John's severed head on a bloody platter!

Imagine *the scene* between Antipas and Herodias after the guests left.

John's disciples took his headless body and buried it. But then Herod Antipas was "perplexed" to learn that what John had been doing—preaching the good news of the Kingdom, healing the sick, and delivering people from demon possession—was happening "everywhere" (Luke 9:6-7).

Imagine the reports of the Twelve when they returned from their mission trip (Mark 6:30; Luke 9:10; compare Matthew 11:1). What do you imagine they had to say?

_____

_____

Antipas was agitated. Why? And why did he want to see Jesus (Luke 9:9)?

_____

_____

A short time later, what part did Herod Antipas play in the ridicule and execution of Jesus (Luke 22:66–23:12; compare Matthew 27:27-31; Mark 15:16-20)?

_____

_____

LEADERSHIP CHALLENGES

What have you discovered about the following:

- Leading with a shortage of workers for the harvest?

  _____

  _____

- Leading while grieving?

  _____

  _____

- Leading in times of great danger?

  _____

  _____

REFLECTION

In reflecting on the Scriptures and insights in this guide, what has been most important for you?

_____

_____

What pressures do you face?

_____

_____

What have you discovered about leading in times of crisis?

_____

_____

SHARING

What will you share with your friends this week?

_____

_____

What can you share with those you are leading to Jesus?

_____

_____

LEADERSHIP AND DEFECTION

THE TWELVE WORKERS returned to report to Jesus. It was a bittersweet experience. They had so much to report, but they were weary, and Jesus was grieving over His cousin's horrific murder. Jesus suggested *time out*, so they launched a boat onto the Sea of Galilee and headed for a "solitary place." Crowds saw them leave, and people "from every town" scrambled along the shore, arriving before them (Mark 6:32-33). Luke records that Jesus "welcomed them and spoke to them about the kingdom of God, and healed those who needed healing" (Luke 9:11).

As evening approached, the disciples became concerned about the crowd, numbering about five thousand men, plus women and children. They were in a "remote place," and the people needed to get food. But Jesus told His disciples: "You give them something to eat" (Mark 6:35-37). They were in for major surprises that evening—experiences of the Kingdom!

READ
  • Matthew 14:13-36; Mark 6:30-56; Luke 9:10-17; John 6:1-71
  • *Messiah*, chapters 39–41

A KINGDOM MEAL

Imagine the mix of people seated on the grass. List who might have been there:

_____

_____

What have you picked up about the mood of the crowd?

_____

_____

What might have been the symbolism of the twelve baskets of leftover food?

_____

_____

In what way did this crowd eating together represent God's Kingdom?

_____

_____

A GATHERING STORM

By the end of the day, Jesus and His disciples were exhausted. The disciples left for Capernaum by boat, while Jesus retreated to the mountains to pray (Matthew 14:22-23; John 6:15-17). He needed time with His Father. There had been no time to grieve, and Jesus had become aware that some "intended to make him king by force" (John 6:14-15). They may have been angry over news of John's death. A major storm was gathering—both on the lake and for His movement!

What indicators do you find that the apostles might have been caught up in the move to make Jesus king? Why had Jesus made them get in the boat, while He dismissed the people (Matthew 14:22-23)?

_____

_____

Imagine the scene. It was dark. A storm was lashing the boat. Out of the darkness and storm walks a man—on the water! Can you blame the apostles for thinking this was a ghost? But what were the real issues? What was going on in their hearts?

_____

_____

Why do you think Jesus was "about to pass by them" (Mark 6:48)?

_____

_____

The apostles' hearts were "hardened" (Mark 6:51-52). What was going on?

_____

_____

Peter left the boat to walk to Jesus. What might this have meant for Jesus?

_____

_____

When Jesus and Peter climbed back into the boat, "the wind died down." How did those in the boat respond (Matthew 14:28-33)?

_____

_____

A MAJOR DEFECTION: CONFUSION OVER BREAD

Attempts to make Jesus king were not only premature, this was not His Kingdom plan. Under Roman oppression, the Jews struggled to survive. They followed Jesus for bread—and what a military leader He would make! He could feed His supporters, heal the wounded, raise the dead, and even walk them across water!

How would you describe the plan Jesus was working with—His own understanding of His mission (John 6:25-71)?

_____

_____

What work did God require of them?

_____

_____

Why were "many of his disciples" offended?

_____

_____

This was a major defection: "From this time many of his disciples turned back and no longer followed him" (John 6:66). The feeding of the five thousand brought this to a head. Jews and Gentiles, slave and free, men, women, and children shared the meal. This illustrated the nature of God's Kingdom, but His Kingdom is not based on "food that spoils" but on "the bread of life"—Jesus Himself.

How do you think the Twelve were feeling at this time (John 6:67-71)?

_____

_____

Notice that it was Peter who spoke. Whatever we might think about Peter being the first to speak, through these storms He had his eyes on Jesus. Mark Edwards observes, "The only way you can 'walk on water' as a leader is to keep your eyes on Jesus."[1]

LEADERSHIP AND DEFECTION

Crowds can overwhelm, and numbers can be intoxicating for movement leaders. It is vitally important to keep perspective, and this is found in prayer with the Father. But how do you handle defections? It is easy to glibly speak of *multiplication by reduction*, but this is painful. Jesus took a stand that saw major defections.

What movement-building principles do you find in Jesus' stand?

_____

_____

Why do numbers not represent a movement? What does represent a movement?

_____

_____

What values are you not prepared to compromise?

_____

_____

REFLECTION

How do you feel when others reject your ideas?

_____

_____

SHARING

What will you share with your friends this week?

_____

_____

What can you share with those you are leading to Jesus?

_____

_____

LEADERSHIP AND PREJUDICE

THE PREVIOUS DAYS had been stressful for Jesus. As well as His cousin's death, He suffered many defections among His disciples when He refused the popular demand to become king. And then Pharisees and teachers of the law arrived from Jerusalem to interrogate Him (Matthew 15:1). The issue this time was what is ceremonially clean and unclean . . . and the bigger issue of who are clean and unclean.

This led Jesus and His disciples on another exciting journey, this time visiting *the unclean*: pagans in Phoenicia on the Mediterranean and then in Roman Decapolis, east of Galilee and the Jordan River. You will see how confronting these experiences were for the Twelve. What lessons did Jesus have for them—and us?

READ
- Matthew 15:1–16:12; Mark 7:1–8:26; John 7:1
- *Messiah*, chapters 42–44

How did Jesus respond to the Pharisees' questions about washing, about clean and unclean?

_____

_____

While Pharisees and teachers focused on external cleanliness (clean hands), Jesus exposed their hearts:

They protected their property and wealth, but neglected aged parents. The command to honor parents was cynically avoided by designating assets that might have provided support as corban, *future offerings for the Temple. In what way did this contrast between their traditions and God's commands expose them as "unclean"?*

_____

_____

What makes people "unclean"?

_____

_____

How does a person become "clean" inside?

_____

_____

Jesus was burning bridges! He was at a turning point in His movement building. Disciples had defected, Pharisees were *offended* (Matthew 15:12), and His Galilean ministry ended abruptly. Matthew says: "Leaving that place, Jesus withdrew to the region of Tyre and Sidon" (Matthew 15:21), the region of Lebanon today.

A Canaanite woman (Matthew 15:21-28; Mark 7:24-30)
How did Jesus' seeming disregard mirror the callous attitude of His disciples?

_____

_____

Pagans "praised the God of Israel" (Matthew 15:29-31; Mark 7:31-37)
Jesus then trekked across the lower Golan to Decapolis, the region of ten Roman cities east of Galilee and the Jordan. People brought to Jesus a deaf man who could hardly speak, and He healed him.

What was the crowd's response (Matthew 15:31)?

_____

_____

A visit to Decapolis (Matthew 15:32-39; Mark 8:1-10)

It was in this region that Jesus had healed a demon-possessed man, telling him, "Go home to your family and tell them how much the Lord has done for you, and how he has had mercy on you." So the man had told "in the Decapolis how much Jesus had done for him. And all the people were amazed" (Mark 5:19-20).

Now, Jesus was back healing in this pagan territory and a large crowd gathered, at least four thousand men, plus women and children.

What suggests that the disciples, who were Jews, struggled to accept these Gentiles?

_____

_____

The yeast of the Pharisees and Herod (Matthew 16:1-12: Mark 8:11-21)

Jesus was weary of the Pharisees' persistent demands for a sign (Mark 8:11-12). Why did He warn His disciples to "watch out for the yeast of the Pharisees and that of Herod" (Mark 8:15, emphasis added)?

_____

_____

Compare the feeding of the five thousand on the western—predominantly Jewish—side of the Sea of Galilee with that of the four thousand on the eastern (pagan) shores:

Who initiated these miracles—and why?

_____

_____

Were the disciples blind to what Jesus was teaching (Mark 8:17-18)?

_____

_____

Why did Jesus draw attention to the number of baskets of leftover food (Matthew 16:9-12; Mark 8:17-21)?

_____

_____

What lesson might Jesus have had in healing a blind man at Bethsaida (Mark 8:22-26)?

_____

_____

It is easy to categorize or even to unintentionally exclude people. What traditions might you follow that leave some as "outsiders"?

_____

_____

With whom do you struggle most to relate: people of other cultures or religions, indigenous people, or migrants?

_____

_____

JESUS MOVED THE FENCES

Toward the end of World War II, a young American soldier was killed in France.[1] His buddies took his body to a nearby French village and approached the local priest for a burial in their cemetery. It was not possible, he explained, because the grounds were fully occupied and it was for Catholics. But he said they could bury their friend in the field next to the cemetery.

Months later, the war ended. The soldiers returned a last time to pay their respects to their friend before leaving for home and a new life. To their dismay, they could not find the gravesite. They were convinced the Catholic priest had desecrated the grave—and they sought him out, with rising anger.

The priest opened the door to their insistent knocking to be confronted by their accusations. In broken English, he explained, "No. I saw your distress and so I did the only thing I could do: I moved the fence. Your friend who was outside is now inside!"

Jesus was moving fences, redefining the Kingdom of God. He was deconstructing the temple system, challenging national boundary markers, and redefining who was in and who was out. His was shifting the boundaries of cultural and religious prejudice, demonstrating that His was a Kingdom of grace for all!

REFLECTION

What new and surprising insights have you gained from this guide?

_____

_____

What prejudices have you discovered in your heart?

_____

_____

SHARING

What will you share with your friends this week?

_____

_____

Identify those you least expect to see in God's Kingdom.

_____

_____

How could you work to share the gospel with some of these people?

_____

_____

What can you share with those you are leading to Jesus?

_____

_____

Why might it be helpful to share prejudices you have discovered in your heart?

_____

_____

LEADERSHIP AND THE ROCK

THE CROWDS WERE AGITATED. Their aspirations for making Jesus king had been thwarted. The Pharisees' attempts to trap Him were frustrated. Warning them to "watch out" for the Pharisees and Herod Antipas (Mark 8:15), Jesus led His disciples across the border into Gaulanitis (the Golan Heights), the territory of tetrarch Philip II. Near Peter and Andrew's hometown of Bethsaida, Jesus healed a blind man, but it was time to retreat.

He took the apostles to the base of Mount Hermon in the region of Caesarea Philippi (Matthew 16:13; Mark 8:27). Caesarea Philippi—also known as Panias or Banias—was built around a cave or grotto from which flowed a major tributary of the Jordan. It was first settled in Greek times, with shrines dedicated to Pan, a nature god. About fifty years before Jesus visited, Herod the Great built a white marble temple at the grotto. In AD 14, his son Philip II had named the city Caesarea Philippi, after himself and Emperor Caesar Augustus. The people there were mostly Gentiles who honored the Roman emperor.[1]

With its scattered villages far from the Jewish heartland and their Kingdom aspirations, this mountainous region provided the perfect retreat for Jesus and His leaders.

READ

- Matthew 16:13–17:13; Mark 8:27–9:13; Luke 9:18-36
- *Messiah*, chapters 45–46

What were the crowds saying about Jesus?

_____

_____

What had Peter come to understand? And what was Jesus' response to his declaration?

_____

_____

For the first recorded time, Jesus used the word church *(ecclesia), an everyday word for a gathering of people in the Greco-Roman world. Why do you think He chose this common, secular term?*

_____

_____

THE FOUNDATION AND HEAD

Jesus is both the foundation of the church and its only head. He declared, "On this rock [*petra*] I will build my church" (Matthew 16:18). "The Christ of God" (Luke 9:20) is the solid foundation rock on which His church is built (1 Corinthians 3:11, 10:4), not on Peter (*petros*), whom Jesus rebuked moments later. The apostles built on this foundation, with Jesus the cornerstone (Ephesians 2:20; 1 Corinthians 3:9; compare 1 Peter 2:4), the one and only head of the church (Ephesians 5:23).

The foundation: In light of recent experiences of Jesus and the disciples, why was this discussion so important?

_____

_____

The head: Jesus spoke of "my church." What does this mean to you?

_____

_____

The temples of Caesarea Philippi represented the gates of Hades—the assault of evil on His people. What would show Jesus' victory over evil (Matthew 16:17-21)?

_____

_____

The church was not the end goal. What understanding of mission do you get from Jesus' words to His disciples: "I will give you the keys of the kingdom of heaven" (Matthew 16:19)?

_____

_____

The truth that He was the Messiah was now out. This was the news the crowds were waiting to hear. Why do you think Jesus told His disciples "not to tell anyone" (Matthew 16:20)?

_____

_____

JESUS BEGAN TO EXPLAIN . . .

Yes, he would go to Jerusalem, but not for military action. Matthew records that "Jesus began to explain to his disciples that he must go to Jerusalem and suffer many things at the hands of the elders, chief priests and teachers of the law, and that he must be killed." They were so shocked that they did not hear His more remarkable statement—"and on the third day be raised to life" (Matthew 16:21).

Their hopes were dashed. What was Peter's response (Matthew 16:22)?

_____

_____

Jesus turned on Peter. Why such a strong reaction (Matthew 16:23)?

_____

_____

His Kingdom is shaped by cruciform love, sacrifice for others, and status reversal. What sacrifice would Jesus' movement demand of disciples (Matthew 16:24-28)?

_____

_____

THE FATHER'S AFFIRMATION

Smarting under Jesus' sharp rebuke, Peter would have found the following days tough. But Jesus sought to draw him closer, choosing Peter, James, and John to climb a high mountain with Him. Some think this was Mount Tabor near Nazareth, others that it was Mount Hermon, near where they had spent the week in retreat. On that mountain, Jesus was "transfigured"—His face shining as the sun, His clothes "as white as the light" (Matthew 17:2), with Moses and Elijah appearing to talk with Him. Just imagine being there!

Peter was so impressed that he suggested building three shelters—one each for Jesus, Moses, and Elijah—but he was interrupted.

What were he and the others told (Matthew 17:1-5)?

_____

_____

REFLECTION

What is the value of retreat and evaluation in movement building?

_____

_____

How do you now understand a disciple-making movement defined by crucifixion?

_____

_____

How do you ensure your life and disciple-making movement is built on Jesus?

_____

_____

What do your shrines to disciple-making movement heroes look like?

_____

_____

After listening to Jesus (Matthew 17:5), what will you obey?

_____

_____

SHARING

What will you share with your friends this week?

_____

_____

How will you use the keys of the gospel to unlock the Kingdom for those you are leading to Jesus?

_____

_____

LEADERSHIP AND TEAM POLITICS

JESUS, PETER, JAMES, AND JOHN came down the mountain to find the other disciples *arguing* with teachers of the law, with a large crowd around them. Jesus asked: "What are you *arguing* with them about?" (Mark 9:16, emphasis added). Then, on the way to Capernaum, Jesus observed tension between his twelve leaders. Once home and in the house, Jesus asked them: "What were you *arguing* about on the road?" (Mark 9:33, emphasis added).

Arguments derail *movements*. Jesus addressed four that cause train wrecks: whom to follow, who is important, who can participate, and how to deal with sinful and hurtful attitudes or actions.

READ
- Matthew 17:14–18:35; Mark 9:14-50; Luke 9:37-50
- *Messiah*, chapters 47–48

1. WHOM DO WE FOLLOW?

The disciples and teachers of the law were arguing about why the disciples couldn't drive a demon out of a boy (Mark 9:14-18). From Jesus' private discussion with His disciples, what do you think the issue was (Mark 9:28-29, compare verses 19-27)?

_____

_____

Jesus had used this idea of little faith before. He was not speaking of a commodity, with a certain quantity needed to purchase God's favor. Rather, some disciples were still unsure of Him. How was their idea of kingdom still blinding their view of the Messiah?

_____

_____

What might Jesus mean by "this mountain" (Matthew 17:20)?

_____

_____

Compare Psalms 2:6, 3:4, 15:1:

_____

_____

Compare Exodus 15:17; Daniel 9:16:

_____

_____

Jesus is Messiah. He does the work of the temple: healing and forgiving! Why do you think He again speaks of His death and resurrection (Matthew 17:22; Mark 9:30-32)?

_____

_____

2. WHO IS THE GREATEST?

Now that they knew Jesus was Messiah, the disciples were plotting for power. Such arguments and deals to gain and maintain status and position paralyze movements.

What insights do you gain from the temple-tax incident (Matthew 17:24-27)?

_____

_____

What do you understand Jesus was saying by drawing attention to a small child among them (Matthew 18:1-14)?

_____

_____

Jesus said, "If anyone wants to be first, he must be the very last, and the servant of all" (Mark 9:35). This attitude of self-denial and sacrifice for others is the supreme value of His Kingdom. He had made the choice of *downward mobility* in becoming human, and now He was on His way to Jerusalem to be crucified as a slave.

How does this cruciform worldview define and shape your life and disciplemaking?

_____

_____

3. WHO CAN PARTICIPATE?

Many wanted to be with Jesus. The Twelve were in the inner circle, even getting private time with Him. When they "saw a man driving out demons" in Jesus' name, they reported back, "We told him to stop, because he was not one of us" (Mark 9:38).

After they had failed in casting out demons (Mark 9:17-18), how do you think they felt when they found others doing this?

_____

_____

Who is on our side? Who is one of us? Who is in and who is out? When can people belong? On what basis will we accept and then affirm them? What are the boundaries? These are challenging but practical questions for movement leaders.

_____

_____

How do you feel about Jesus' response, and what might be the implications for you (Mark 9:39-41)?

_____

_____

4. WHO DEALS WITH SINFUL CONDUCT?

The Kingdom of God is not hierarchical. It reflects God's triune nature, His love and sacrifice for others. But some pursue their own interests, hurting and offending. Jesus outlined a process to follow when one person sins against another.

What type of sinful, self-interested conduct is Jesus speaking of (Matthew 18:15-20)?

_____

_____

How do you understand this process working?

_____

_____

Emotional triangles are part of human behavior.[1] They can be neutral, but also destructive. For example, if a person feels aggrieved or *sinned against*, complaining to a third party creates further rifts and tensions, often destroying people and movements.

Who is to deal with offensive, sinful attitudes or behaviors?

_____

_____

How does this avoid destructive triangles from spiraling out of control?

_____

_____

INTERPERSONAL POLITICS

How are the four issues Jesus addressed significant to you as a disciplemaker?

_____

_____

Politics play a big part in churches and denominations today: Who will be in control? Who will hold position? And who can be a member? What do you think might have been Jesus' idea of church?

_____

_____

SHARING

What will you share with your friends this week?

_____

_____

What can you share with those you are leading to Jesus?

_____

_____

WHAT WAS JESUS' IDEA
OF CHURCH?

WHAT SORT OF MOVEMENT was Jesus developing? How did this reflect His cruciform worldview?[1] And, what was His understanding of church? How does it compare with what has evolved over the centuries?

Matthew is the only Gospel writer who records Jesus using the word *ecclesia* (*church*). Affirming Peter's declaration that He was the divine Christ, Jesus spoke of "my church" (Matthew 16:18). Then, outlining a process for resolving tensions when one person *sins against* another, He involved "the church" (Matthew 18:17). We will reflect again on the context of these words to ask: What was Jesus' idea of church? Why is this important for disciplemakers and the movement Jesus was building?

READ
- Matthew 16:13–18:35

What are some of the features you have discovered about Jesus' idea of church (Matthew 16:13-21, 18:15-20)?

The word *church* is a translation of a common Greek word (*ecclesia*), used since the fifth century BC to describe citizens gathering to decide on matters concerning their welfare. Translators of the Septuagint—a Greek translation of the Old Testament, completed in the second century BC—used this word to refer to Israelites assembling before God, but it was not a religious or political term and never referred to a building. Later, it would become Paul's favorite way of referring to Christian communities.[2]

From the time Jesus first called His disciples *my church* or *gathering*—having openly confirmed his identity as "the Christ, the Son of the living God"—Jesus "began to explain" to them that "he must be killed and on the third day be raised to life" (Matthew 16:16, 18, 21).

In Matthew 16:16-19, Jesus spoke of building a worldwide community of followers. The next time He used the word *church* (Matthew 18:15-20), He spoke of a local, gathered community. This is the beauty of the word *ecclesia* as redefined by Jesus. His community of believers is at one and the same time universal and local.

In what ways did Jesus define His Kingdom movement by His crucifixion?

_____

_____

How is the purpose of church shaped by its relationship to Kingdom (Matthew 16:19)?

_____

_____

Try to imagine a cruciform church. What might a gathering molded by the attitude that led Jesus to the cross look like?

_____

_____

GOD'S MISSION

Mission originates with God and flows from His heart.[3] He was the first missionary. It is His activity. It is His very nature as the God of "the other." Even within the triune being of God, the other is always the concern of each divine Person. God's nature is to save the lost—to bring all people back into His realm and relationship: "For God so loved the world that he gave his one and only Son, that whoever believes in him shall not perish but have eternal life. For God did not send his Son into the world to condemn the world, but to save the world through him" (John 3:16-17).

Jesus' mission is God's mission. Imagine and describe what church might look like if shaped by each of these realities:

- *His mission:* to share the good news of the Kingdom—releasing, healing, delivering

  _____

  _____

- *His attitude:* considering the interests of others more important than His own

  _____

  _____

- *His incarnation:* becoming human, identifying with our limitations and circumstances

  _____

  _____

- *His anointing:* by the Holy Spirit, fully human and fully God, with no dichotomy

  _____

  _____

- *His method:* mingling, sympathizing, meeting needs, and inviting people to follow Him

  _____

  _____

- *His invitations:* to all, to be disciples—who make other disciples

  _____

  _____

- *His sacrifice:* a slave, the Lamb on "the eternal cross,"[4] revealing God's cruciform nature

  _____

  _____

In what ways do you perceive church has changed since New Testament times?

_____

_____

CHURCH FOR POST-CHRISTIAN AND POSTMODERN TIMES (PHILIPPIANS 2:1-11)

What is the value of conversational rather than hierarchical leadership?

_____

_____

How do the methods of a church define its message?

_____

_____

In contrast to bounded-set, what might Christ-centered church look like?

_____

_____

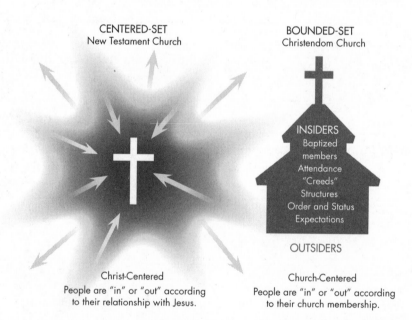

CENTERED-SET
New Testament Church

BOUNDED-SET
Christendom Church

INSIDERS
Baptized
members
Attendance
"Creeds"
Structures
Order and Status
Expectations

OUTSIDERS

Christ-Centered
People are "in" or "out" according
to their relationship with Jesus.

Church-Centered
People are "in" or "out" according
to their church membership.

REFLECTION

Why do you think many are disillusioned with church?

_____

_____

What might you do about it?

_____

_____

SHARING

What will you share with your friends this week?

_____

_____

What can you share with those you are leading to Jesus?

_____

_____

ESSENTIALS SHARED PLAINLY AND OPENLY

JESUS HAD WORKED tirelessly to transform His apostles' worldview, to embrace loving sacrifice for others, even their enemies. It was now time to openly demonstrate the extent of such love (John 13:1), and Luke writes: "Jesus resolutely set out for Jerusalem" (Luke 9:51).

John's Gospel records three visits to Jerusalem: first, for the Feast of Tabernacles (John 7:2); second, the Feast of Dedication (John 10:22); and then His final Passover (John 12:1).

In this guide, we explore Jesus' experiences at the first two. On these journeys, Jesus faced ridicule—Jerusalem was "the home ground of his strongest enemies"[1]—but He shared openly. So what did He disclose concerning the undergirding principles and foundations of His movement?

READ
  • Matthew 8:19-22; Luke 9:51-62; John 7:2–10:24
  • *Messiah*, chapters 49–52

On His way to Jerusalem, what reception did Jesus receive in Samaria? How did His apostles react (Luke 9:52-56)?

How did Jesus illustrate that total commitment was required
(Luke 9:57-62)?

_____

_____

In what ways did His brothers' expectations differ from His? And why
(John 7:2-9)?

_____

_____

THE FEAST OF TABERNACLES

With the grain, olives, and grapes harvested and the agricultural year
ended (Exodus 23:16), Jewish men were expected in Jerusalem. After His
brothers left, Jesus, who had avoided confrontation by not attending all
feasts, went "in secret," arriving halfway through the week (John 7:10-14).

For this seven-day festival, families lived in booths (*sukkôth*) made
of branches, reminiscent of their wilderness days (Leviticus 23:33-43).
Four large candelabras in the Women's Court of the temple radiated light
across the city.[2] Early each morning, worshippers carrying willow branches
circled the altar of burnt offerings, while others joined a procession of
priests carrying water from the Pool of Siloam up the steep Herodian
Street from the Kidron Valley, dancing and chanting, "With joy you will
draw water from the wells of salvation" (Isaiah 12:3).

On the seventh and last day, crowds surged around the altar seven
times with branches and water. The water was then mixed with sacrificial
wine and poured into a conduit to flow back into the Kidron Valley.[3] The
festive spirit, the vigorous processions, and the warm September–October
weather left the crowds of pilgrims exhausted.

In alluding to this "water drawing" ceremony and the crowd's exhaustion,
what invitations did Jesus make (John 7:37-39; compare Isaiah 55:1-3)?

_____

_____

While some were divided over Jesus' comments, the chief priests and Pharisees
were angry. At the high point of the festival, before the "mob" they considered
ignorant of the law (John 7:49), Jesus had challenged their authority.

THE VALIDITY OF JESUS' TESTIMONY (JOHN 7:53–8:59)

By the next day, in a dramatic and public confrontation, the teachers of the law and Pharisees posed a question of interpretation by which to humiliate Jesus, intending to destroy His growing influence and popularity.

How did the teachers and Pharisees frame their "trap" (John 7:53–8:11)?

According to Josephus, on feast days, Roman soldiers patrolled the crowd and the long, covered walkway constructed by Herod the Great on three sides of the vast Temple enclosure. So Jesus' response was observed by an armed military presence.[4]

The eighth day of the feast was treated as a Sabbath, with no work (Leviticus 23:33-44). The rabbis defined writing as work, with writing defined as "making some kind of permanent mark like putting ink on paper." Writing in dust was permissible, for it left "no lasting mark."[5] It is obvious that Jesus knew their laws and interpretations.

Imagine the woman's shame and terror, and the injustice of the situation: Where is the man? What is the evidence that this was a trap? And what options did Jesus have?

Jesus could have written "kill her" or "stone her,"[6] but the Roman authorities denied Jews the right to put people to death (John 18:31). Sometimes they did (Acts 7:57-60), but not in the temple courts with soldiers watching. Violence would have resulted in the imprisonment of Jesus.

The Pharisees wanted the strict application of the law; Jesus fought for justice—even in saying, "If any one of you is without sin, let him be the first to throw a stone at her" (John 8:7). In the Middle East, the crowd would look to the oldest present to lead, but instead they left![7]

How did Jesus' allusions to the candelabras flooding the city with light testify to His mission as Savior? On what basis would the requirements of the law with its death penalty be met so that he could say, "Then neither do I condemn you. . . . Go now and leave your life of sin" (reread John 8:12-59)?

THE CLAIMS OF JESUS DEMONSTRATED (JOHN 9:1-41)

Jesus met a blind man on the road. This gave Him the opportunity to display the work of God (John 9:4). Mark Edwards suggests tracing and comparing[8] . . .

The progression of the blind man receiving sight:

- Verse 1:
- Verse 11:
- Verse 17:
- Verse 27:
- Verse 33:
- Verse 38:

The progression of the Pharisees becoming blind:

- Verse 15:
- Verse 16:
- Verse 24:
- Verses 28-29:
- Verse 34:
- Verse 39:

It was a Sabbath. In what way did this aggravate His accusers and, at the same time, demonstrate Jesus' authority?

How did Jesus' declarations that "I am the gate for the sheep" and "I am the good shepherd" further divide His accusers (John 10:1-21)?

THE FEAST OF LIGHTS (JOHN 10:22-42)

We cannot be certain of the precise sequence of events. While Jesus might have stayed around Jerusalem for some time after the Feast of Tabernacles,[9] Gospel harmonies suggest He left the city to return in winter for the Feast of Dedication—also known as the Festival of Lights.[10] In his Gospel, John tells the story of this visit following the healing of the blind man.

This festival came ten weeks after Tabernacles, celebrating the purification of the temple by Judas Maccabeus in 164 BC, exactly three years after its defilement by Antiochus Epiphanes.[11] Each evening during this eight-day winter festival, when Jerusalem could be covered in snow, another light was lit on the eight-armed Hanukkah lamp.[12]

Like lights being lit, Jesus plainly revealed something about Himself at this feast. What was it (John 10:22-42)?

JESUS' MOVEMENT

What essential principles did Jesus openly and plainly underscore by:

- Alluding to the "water drawing" ceremony at the Tabernacles Feast (John 7:37-39)?

- Personally suffering the costly consequences of the woman's sin (John 7:53–8:11)?

- Healing the blind man on the Sabbath (John 9:1–10:21)?

- Plainly telling all "in the temple area" at the Feast of Dedication: "I give [my sheep] eternal life" and "I and the Father are one" (John 10:22-42)?

REFLECTION
What has surprised you in this section?

_____

_____

SHARING
What will you share with your friends this week?

_____

_____

What can you share with those you are leading to Jesus?

_____

_____

THE *PERSON OF PEACE* AND STEPS TO MULTIPLICATION

DURING THE THREE MONTHS between the Feast of Tabernacles (John 7:2) and His return in winter for the Feast of Dedication (John 10:22), Jesus was most likely in Judea, never far from Jerusalem. Luke provides the narrative.

It was an intense time of leadership multiplication. Appointing the seventy-two (or seventy), Jesus repeated much of what He had previously shared in training the Twelve. By examining His succinct, practical instruction in disciplemaking and movement building, we gain insight into how we might also multiply leaders.

READ
- Luke 10:1-24
- *Messiah*, chapter 53

Jesus saw the potential of a large harvest. How does such a vision define our attitude?

How did Jesus identify people of peace, and what part do they play in movements?

- _____
- _____
- _____

Because of their *reputation*—either good or bad—such people have wide *influence* in sharing, as did the Samaritan woman (John 4:1-42) and Zacchaeus (Luke 19:1-10).

What practical insights did Jesus give for connecting with people and making disciples?

_____

_____

Why was Jesus so excited by the reports of the seventy-two? What had they discovered through involvement in His mission?

_____

_____

FOUR FIELDS + SIX STEPS TO MULTIPLICATION

Using an overlay of the *four fields harvest model* (Mark 4:26-29) and Jesus' teaching on how to enter new fields and make disciples (Luke 10:1-24), we identify six steps to planting multiplying *gatherings* of new disciples—new groups or churches.[1]

1. Pray for the harvest and workers. (Luke 10:1-4)

What was Jesus' specific instruction for prayer?

_____

_____

How and with whom do you pray this prayer?

_____

_____

2. Connect through the "person of peace." (Luke 10:5-9, 16)
Why is this person key to relational streams?

_____

_____

What do you think of Jesus' plan to engage with people?

_____

_____

- *Eat* their food—and, while you do, listen to *their story*, identifying their needs.
- *Heal* their hurts—perhaps briefly relating *your story* as a bridge to God.
- *Introduce* Jesus—your testimony can connect to *Jesus' story*.

Jesus was always on the lookout for new disciples. He followed these three steps to engage, equip, and release people. As an example, reflect on the indicators that Zacchaeus was a potential *person of peace*.

How did Jesus engage him and his influence for His movement of disciplemaking once he became a disciple (Luke 19:1-10)?

_____

_____

Try it out: Look for an opportunity to eat or drink with someone this week. Focus on listening to their story and sympathizing with their hurts or needs. In one sentence, share your testimony—and perhaps introduce God's story.

Who will you do this with this week?

_____

_____

3. Sow gospel seed, announcing that "the Kingdom of God is near." (Luke 10:9)
How might gospel seed be sown so that the growth does not depend on you?

_____

_____

Discovery Bible Reading[2] is a simple, effective plan, whatever your level of knowledge or experience of Jesus:

- Friends meet to read a Gospel (Mark's Gospel is a good place to start).
- Start reading at the beginning—one story at a time.
- Read each story through twice, then retell the story in your own words.
- Discuss using five bookmark questions:

  1. What is new?
  2. What surprises you?
  3. What don't you understand?
  4. What will you obey or apply?
  5. What will you share with another person this week?

4. Grow—through service, making disciples, and the Word.

Using the same *Discovery Bible Reading* approach, a group of friends could read other Bible books, while also getting involved in community initiatives and engaging with disadvantaged people, as Jesus did.

5. Gather people who are part of the relational stream—and invite others to join.

Who are the natural facilitators?

_____

_____

In what ways might you share food, fellowship, service, and worship?

_____

_____

Read Acts—an inspiring *manual* on multiplying new groups and churches—using the five bookmark questions as a basis for application and obedience.

6. Multiply into new relational streams.

Jesus laid the foundations of a sustainable and multiplying movement. What was He sharing and handing on?

_____

_____

Who are you equipping to multiply, to start another group?

_____

_____

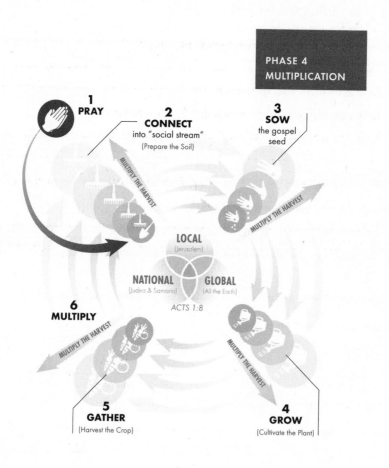

REFLECTION

Jesus explained His own practice in making disciples. His approach proves effective in whatever social context we find ourselves—modern or post-modern, Christendom or post-Christendom, spiritual or secular.

How might Jesus' instruction for disciplemaking and multiplication relate to your context?

_____

_____

SHARING

What will you share with your friends this week?

_____

_____

What can you share with those you are leading to Jesus?

_____

_____

Are you ready to "gather" as a group of disciples? Is this the beginning of a new church? What could this look like?

_____

_____

JESUS' RADICAL
WORLDVIEW AFFIRMED

THE INSTRUCTION AND EXPERIENCES Jesus gave the seventy-two were similar to those He had shared when equipping His twelve apostles. Were some of them with Him during the intense weeks of teaching leading up to the winter Feast of Dedication in Jerusalem? Was He multiplying His inner leadership team?

During this time, Jesus was in Judea, never far from Jerusalem, with a visit to Bethany on the eastern slopes of the Mount of Olives. There is a sense of urgency. Jesus was open and direct, even confrontational. It was one training session after another. In these, He affirmed His radical, upside-down, sacrificial worldview.

READ
- Luke 10:25–13:21
- *Messiah*, chapter 54

Jesus' fourth invitation is "Love your enemies." How do the following experiences demonstrate the radical nature of God and His worldview of status reversal?

- My neighbor (Luke 10:25-37)—the most unlikely:

_____

_____

- My priorities (Luke 10:38-42)—disregard taboos:

_____

_____

- My prayers (Luke 11:1-13)—Holy Spirit dependence:

_____

_____

- My response (Luke 11:14-36)—"hear the word of God and obey it":

_____

_____

- My religion (Luke 11:37-54):

_____

_____

- My authenticity (Luke 12:1-12):

_____

_____

How did Jesus' warnings further illustrate His radical worldview?

_____

_____

- Greed and wealth (Luke 12:13-34):

_____

_____

- Faithfulness and wisdom (Luke 12:35-48):

_____

_____

- Family divisions (Luke 12:49-53):

_____

_____

- Discernment (Luke 12:54-59):

_____

_____

- Judgments (Luke 13:1-9):

_____

_____

BRINGING IT TOGETHER!

Before returning to Jerusalem for the Feast of Dedication Jesus boldly healed a cripple in a synagogue on the Sabbath and then shared two parables to explain the nature of the Kingdom of God (Luke 13:10-21).

In what way did this Sabbath miracle illustrate His worldview?

_____

_____

How did the mustard seed planted by a man illustrate His Kingdom?

_____

_____

What do we learn about His Kingdom from women working yeast into dough?

_____

_____

Review the confrontation at the Feast of Dedication. What did Jesus plainly reveal, illustrating the nature of His movement by His incarnation (John 10:22-39)?

_____

_____

BOTH MEN AND WOMEN

The parable of the mustard seed—men farming—is linked with the story of women kneading leaven into bread dough. Kenneth Bailey identifies twenty-seven examples of this kind of pairing in Luke's Gospel: a story relating to men, another to women. Further examples include:[1]

- In His Luke 4 sermon in Nazareth, Jesus told of the faith of the widow of Zarephath, as well as that of Namaan.
- In Luke 5, Jesus presented twin parables: the mending of a garment (the task of women at that time) and the making of wine (the work of men).
- In Luke 15, the parable of a man searching for his lost sheep is told together with that of a woman turning her house upside down to find a lost coin, perhaps her dowry.

Jesus created parables and shared stories of men and women, for He was making disciples of both.

REFLECTION

For you, what has been most important about the radical nature of God revealed by Jesus?

_____

_____

SHARING

What will you share with your friends this week about Jesus' worldview?

_____

_____

What can you share with those you are leading to Jesus?

_____

_____

JESUS' KEY DISCIPLEMAKING PRINCIPLES AFFIRMED

ANOTHER ATTEMPT WAS MADE on Jesus' life at the Feast of Dedication. While walking in Solomon's Colonnade in the Temple area, some Jews cornered Him, demanding, "How long will you keep us in suspense? If you are the Christ, tell us plainly" (John 10:24).

Angered by His response that His miracles testified to the truth of His declaration that "I and the Father are one," they "picked up stones to stone him." They "tried to seize him," but he "escaped their grasp" and "went back across the Jordan" to Perea, "where John had been baptizing in the early days" (John 10:25-40). He stayed there about three months. The welcome He received there was in stark contrast to the threats He had escaped in Jerusalem—and "many believed" (John 10:42).

While on the move, even as He headed back toward Jerusalem the final time, with detours into Samaria and Galilee, Jesus reviewed the essentials of this multiplication phase of movement building: key disciplemaking principles, the radical nature of His Kingdom worldview, and lessons in leadership multiplication.

READ
- Luke 13:22–17:10; John 10:40–11:54
- *Messiah*, chapters 55–59

PRINCIPLES FOR DISCIPLEMAKERS

1. It is the unlikely who become disciples. (Luke 13:22-30)

Jesus taught that "people will come from east and west and north and south, and will take their places at the feast in the kingdom of God. Indeed there are those who are last who will be first, and first who will be last" (Luke 13:29-30).

What preconceptions or prejudices blind you to welcoming, equipping, and releasing the most unlikely as disciples?

---

2. It takes determination with compassion to make disciples. (Luke 13:31-35)

Nothing could distract Jesus from making disciples, yet there was no hardness of attitude. He grieved: "O Jerusalem, Jerusalem . . . how often I have longed to gather your children together . . . but you were not willing!" (Luke 13:34-35).

How do you find the balance between determination and compassionate identification with people in your disciplemaking?

---

3. Don't do it for reward. (Luke 14:1-24)

When He appointed the Twelve, Jesus explained that if you do religious deeds for the accolades of others, this will be the only reward you get (Matthew 6:1-18). Now, invited to the home of a "prominent Pharisee" on a Sabbath, Jesus challenged His hosts.

Do you seek honor for disciplemaking? Who are you investing in— the successful and those who can applaud you, or those who are broken and cannot repay you?

---

4. Be honest; it is costly. (Luke 14:25-35)

Being a disciple and making disciples is costly. Being a disciple can cost family and friends, for it is a *cruciform* choice and lifestyle. Jesus put it this way: "Anyone who does not carry his cross and follow me cannot be my disciple" (Luke 14:27).

Count the cost! What has been the reality for you, in being a disciple and in making disciples?

_____

_____

5. It is among the lost where disciples are found. (Luke 15:1-32)

It is from the lost that disciples are made. Jesus told three parables affirming their value—the lost sheep, coin, and men—three times declaring that there is great celebration and rejoicing over the lost being found (Luke 15:7, 10, 32).

The lost are found in uncomfortable, dirty, and dangerous situations, as well as our homes, workplaces, and churches. Where do you spend your time making disciples?

_____

_____

Reflect on whether you regularly eat with people who don't yet know Jesus. Do "sinners" seek your company? If so, how does this happen?

_____

_____

6. Your service cannot be divided. (Luke 16:1-31)

Jesus talked with His disciples about the "unfaithful but shrewd manager" (Luke 16:1-13) and responded to the sneers of the Pharisees about the dangers of wealth with the story of "the rich man and Lazarus" (Luke 16:14-31).

However shrewd we think we are, "No servant can serve two masters"—
God and money. What might we "highly value" that is "detestable in God's
sight" (Luke 16:15)?

_____

_____

7. Don't "let the side down."[1] (Luke 17:1-10)
What contrast do you identify between faith and duty?

_____

_____

What are the implications for leaders in disciplemaking and movement
building?

_____

_____

8. Don't be surprised by where the opposition comes from. (John 11:1-16)
Religious leaders get jealous. They sometimes don't appreciate the success
of others, unless it honors them. So don't expect that if you bring new
life to a community, revival to a church—even raising the dead—that the
Pharisees will be pleased!

What was it that compelled Jesus to return to Bethany, despite the risk?

_____

_____

9. Be wise: There are times to withdraw. (John 11:45-54)
What signaled it was time to withdraw to Ephraim?

_____

_____

SHARING
What will you share with your friends who are on this journey with you?

_____

_____

In what way has this leadership multiplication phase impacted you?

_____

_____

How has your life been changed by this multiplication phase?

_____

_____

As a result of exploring this phase of Jesus' disciplemaking and movement building, how do you relate to those you are encouraging to know and follow Jesus as disciples?

_____

_____

THE LAST COME FIRST

RAISING HIS FRIEND LAZARUS to life frustrated the Temple authorities. A meeting of the Sanhedrin was called. "'What are we accomplishing?' they asked. 'Here is this man performing many miraculous signs. If we let him go on like this, everyone will believe in him, and then the Romans will come and take away both our place and our nation.'"

Caiaphas was annoyed: "You know nothing at all!" he remonstrated. "You do not realize that it is better for you that one man die for the people than that the whole nation perish." John records that "from that day on they plotted to take his life. Therefore Jesus no longer moved about publicly among the Jews" but withdrew to Ephraim in northern Judea,[1] on the edge of the desert, close to the borders of Samaria and Galilee (John 11:47-54).

During these dangerous times, Jesus continued to equip His disciples (Luke 17:22, 18:1). You will notice that a common theme was that the last—the humble, sinners, little children, servants, and slaves—shall be first!

READ
- Luke 17:11–19:28; Matthew 19:1–20:34; Mark 10:1-52
- *Messiah*, chapters 60–61

What essential frames for movement leaders did Jesus press home?

- Coping with ingratitude (Luke 17:11-19):

  _____

  _____

- Understanding the nature of His Kingdom movement
  (Luke 17:20-37):

  _____

  _____

- Persistent reliance on God (Luke 18:1-8):

  _____

  _____

- The folly of confidence in one's own righteousness (Luke 18:9-14):

  _____

  _____

ESCAPE TO PEREA

With His disciples and large crowds following, Jesus crossed to the eastern side of the Jordan River valley into Perea, where the mountains rise steeply to the desert beyond. Herod Antipas, ruler of Galilee, also ruled Perea, which is the region of Mount Nebo and the fortified hilltop palace of Machaerus, where it is believed John the Baptist was executed.

What lessons did Jesus have for His disciples or movement leaders in these stories?

- Pharisees came to test Jesus (Matthew 19:1-12; Mark 10:1-12):

  What was the lesson for His disciples?

  _____

  _____

- Little children were brought for blessing (Matthew 19:13-15; Mark 10:13-16; Luke 18:15-17):

  What was Jesus teaching His movement leaders?

  _____

  _____

- A rich young ruler came seeking eternal life (Matthew 18:16-30; Mark 10:17-31; Luke 18:18-30):

  How did Jesus relate this experience to His movement leaders?

  _____

  _____

- In what ways does the parable of the landowner's sovereignty demonstrate the radical nature of God's Kingdom (Matthew 20:1-16)?

  _____

  _____

THE ROAD TO DEATH

With Passover drawing near, Jesus crossed back over the Jordan River, heading toward Jericho to traverse the rugged Wadi Qelt up to Jerusalem. The road through Jericho led close to the theater Herod the Great had constructed for the entertainment of his guests, perhaps under the aqueduct bringing water to the pools of his winter palace. In Jesus' time, this agricultural center—with a wide variety of fruit and extensive date plantations—was "a winter resort for Jerusalem's aristocracy."[2]

At some place, he took the Twelve aside, confiding in them that He would be betrayed, mocked, flogged, and crucified in Jerusalem—but raised to life three days later! This is the third time Jesus had predicted His death,[3] but they were confused: "They did not know what he was talking about" (Matthew 20:17-19; Mark 10:32-34; Luke 18:31-34).

Again, three incidents—two near Jericho—and a parable are recorded from this last journey. What essential insights do you gain into Jesus' Kingdom movement?

- A request for political status (Matthew 20:20-28; Mark 10:35-45):

  In light of Jesus' predictions of death, this was a strange request. What radical principle did Jesus highlight (Matthew 20:25-26)?

  _____

  _____

- A desperate plea for sight (Matthew 20:29-34; Mark 10:46-52; Luke 18:35-43):

    What were the lessons for His disciples?

    _____

    _____

- A climb to see Jesus (Luke 19:1-10):

    On the road to His crucifixion, Jesus was still making and equipping disciples. Zacchaeus was a classic person of peace—receptive, hospitable, with a reputation and influence (Luke 10:5-9). Upsetting the crowd, Jesus stayed at his house. Why? What was Jesus saying?

    _____

    _____

- The parable Jesus told reflected the violence of rulers in His day. (Luke 19:11-27)

    Why do you think He shared this story?

    _____

    _____

    What do you think might be the important Kingdom principles shown in this parable, given that not every detail is to be applied literally?

    _____

    _____

ARRIVAL IN BETHANY

Jesus arrived in Bethany six days before Passover (John 12:1). The crowds arriving for the festival were looking out for Him in the Temple courts; priests and Pharisees were watching to arrest Him (John 11:55-57). By the end of the week, Jesus would be crucified outside Jerusalem.

Bethany is just over the ridge, on the steep eastern slopes of the Mount of Olives—only two miles away but out of sight of Jerusalem. Archaeologist and Qumran researcher Yigael Yadin identified Bethany as one of the three villages east of Jerusalem, mentioned in the Temple Scroll, "in which Essene lepers and those afflicted with other impurities were allowed to settle."[4] They were not permitted to go into the city or Temple area (Leviticus 13:45-46). Bethany's location east of the Temple—as well as the village of Bethphage, a little further up the ridge—provided the perfect settlement for them.

It was here in Bethany that Jesus would be invited to the home of Simon the leper for a meal in His honor. It was at this banquet that, with her sister Martha serving guests and her brother Lazarus, who had been raised from the dead, reclining with the men, Mary took the opportunity to anoint Jesus' feet with expensive perfume (Matthew 26:6-13; Mark 14:3-9; John 12:2-8).[5]

REFLECTION

Jesus had labored tirelessly to equip multiplying leaders. His focus had been on transforming their worldview, for His Kingdom movement is founded on sacrificial love, even for enemies. It is a *movement through sacrifice!*

Survey guides 23–40 and identify what you believe are essential frames for Jesus' movement building from this leadership multiplication phase:

- _____
- _____
- _____
- _____
- _____
- _____
- _____
- _____
- _____
- _____
- _____

In what ways has the direction of His ministry surprised you?

_____

_____

To what extent have you incorporated Jesus' movement-building approach in your life?

_____

_____

SHARING

In what way has this leadership multiplication phase influenced and impacted you?

_____

_____

As a result of exploring the first four phases of Jesus' life and disciplemaking, how are you now relating to those you are encouraging to know and follow Jesus as disciples?

_____

_____

Movements

THROUGH HOLY SPIRIT ANOINTING

JESUS HAD an impeccable sense of timing. When urged by His brothers to attend the Feast of Tabernacles, Jesus responded, "The right time for me has not yet come" (John 7:6, compare verse 8). When in Jerusalem—for that feast—His enemies "tried to seize him, but no one laid a hand on him, because his time had not yet come" (John 7:30, compare John 8:20). But six months later, He arrived in Jerusalem saying, "My appointed time is near" (Matthew 26:18). He announced that "the hour has come for the Son of Man to be glorified" (John 12:23), and by the Thursday evening of that week, "Jesus knew that the time had come for him to leave this world and go to the Father" (John 13:1). It was that night that He prayed, "Father, the time has come" (John 17:1).

The time had come for all to see the fullest revelation of what God is like, for Him to be lifted up in death for our salvation, "for the Son of Man to be glorified." And it was time for His movement to go viral—so it was time to leave.[1] Jesus said, "I tell you the truth, unless a kernel of wheat falls to the ground and dies, it remains only a single seed. But if it dies, it produces many seeds. The man who loves his life will lose it, while the man who hates his life in this world will keep it for eternal life" (John 12:23-25). To transform His ministry into a viral movement of *disciples who make disciples who make disciples*, He must stare down the risk of its extinction in His death.[2]

Jesus took sacrifice to its ultimate end, demonstrating the radical nature of His worldview, giving up His life for others. Then, following His resurrection, He appeared to His disciples, saying, "'As the Father has sent me, I am sending you.' And with that he breathed on them, and said, 'Receive the Holy Spirit'" (John 20:21-22). This fifth invitation wasn't specifically articulated until after Jesus' resurrection, but it pervades the experiences of the week leading to His death.

His arrival in Jerusalem and final week could be viewed as the transition to the fifth phase of Jesus' ministry, the *viral movement* phase, in which His body of disciples multiply disciplemaking for His Kingdom. This period covers sections 128–184 in *The NIV Harmony of the Gospels* and chapters 62–87 in *Messiah*. The guides for this phase of Jesus' ministry begin with His entry into Jerusalem as King (*Messiah*, chapter 63), placing His anointing by Mary (chapter 62) later in the week. They culminate with Christ blessing His disciples and His departure (Mark 16:19-20; Luke 24:50-53; Acts 1:1-12).

Jesus began His disciplemaking following His baptism by the Spirit, and His disciples—as His *body*—would now be baptized with the same Spirit for the same work. He was stepping away; His movement was to go *viral*.

Luke's second letter—the Book of Acts—tells the story of what followed. But Jesus' teachings and experiences leading to His crucifixion and resurrection underscore the essentials of this Kingdom movement. What did Jesus focus on in that final week? Why was it so important that His *method* of movement building reflect His *message* of salvation, of drawing people into relationship with God and eternal life? And how did His final invitation lay the foundations for an explosion of disciplemaking?

FRUITFULNESS

Who Gives a Fig?

WHAT DID JESUS do on Palm Sunday for His Kingdom movement to go viral?[1] And why did He curse a flourishing fig tree the next day? Why such dramatic scenes in the Temple? Within the week, He would be crucified. What vital movement principle was He teaching?

READ
- Matthew 21:1-22; Mark 11:1-25; Luke 19:29-48, 21:37-38; John 11:55–12:50
- *Messiah*, chapters 63–65, 68

The crowds preparing for the Passover in Jerusalem were on the lookout for Jesus. The chief priests and Pharisees had given orders that "if anyone found out where Jesus was, he should report it so that they might arrest him" (John 11:57). Hearing He had arrived in Bethany, a large crowd went out to see Him. They also wanted to see Lazarus, whom Jesus had raised. His resurrection was causing quite a stir: the catalyst for many to follow Jesus, inspiring the priests to plot to kill both men (John 12:10-11). The time had come for Jesus to publicly enter Jerusalem as Messiah and King.

THE KING WEEPS OVER JERUSALEM

With a large crowd around Him, Jesus climbed the steep eastern slopes of the Mount of Olives. He sent two disciples ahead to the village of Bethphage to get His "royal mount."

What do we learn of Jesus the King and His Kingdom from the following features of this story?

- The mount He chose, hardly a prancing royal warhorse:

  _____

  _____

- The welcome of the Jerusalem crowd, with palm branches of righteous victory:

  _____

  _____

- The "royal" garments laid out for Him, those of the poor:

  _____

  _____

- The tears, agony, and despair He expressed as the city and Temple came into view:

  _____

  _____

- The crowds who joyfully welcomed Him—the blind, lame, and children:

  _____

  _____

Descending the Mount of Olives and crossing the Kidron Valley, Jesus entered Jerusalem's Temple courts by the east gate—the gate of priests and kings. It was late. He looked around, then left with His twelve apostles, returning to Bethany—perhaps to the home of Lazarus, Mary, and Martha, or to "the hill called the Mount of Olives" (Luke 21:37).

THE KING LOOKS FOR FRUIT

Early the next day, Jesus headed back into the city. "He was hungry"— and went looking for food (Matthew 21:18-19; Mark 11:12-13). What kind of king was He? What fruit was He seeking? Mark tells the story in three parts, with the condition of the fig tree bracketing the other events of the day.[2]

1. *The fig tree (Mark 11:12-14)*

It was not the season for figs, but a fig tree in full leaf caught Jesus' eye. It was large and impressive: He saw it "in the distance." What frustrated Him about it?

_____

_____

2. *The Temple (Mark 11:15-18)*

The Temple and its services were also impressive. In what ways did His search for fruit become a fitting parable of the Temple, chief priests, and teachers of the law?

_____

_____

In these same Temple courts, Jesus had declared Himself to be the one-man temple (John 2:18-22). For more than three years, He had done the work of the Temple across Judea, Galilee, and into pagan lands—healing and forgiving. He was back, doing the same. Who welcomed Him (Matthew 21:12-16)?

_____

_____

3. *The fig tree (Mark 11:19-25)*

The fruit Jesus sought was found neither on the fig tree nor in the Temple system. Rather than outward display—impressive growth, structures, and buildings—what is paramount to His Kingdom movement?

_____

_____

UNEXPECTED FRUIT AND INCONGRUOUS GLORY

Tension was high in the Temple courts: tables overturned, money scattered, the Temple authorities irate and looking to kill Jesus, the whole crowd "amazed at his teaching" (Mark 11:18). Amid this confusion, some Greeks approached the disciples, wanting to "see Jesus" (John 12:20-50). They could not come near Herod's temple. Beyond the outer court for women was another for Gentiles, then the city walls through which lepers could not enter. But instead of treating women, Gentiles, or lepers as unclean and forbidding them to draw near to God, Jesus went to them, granting access to the Father and dismantling the establishment.[3]

What was His response when He learned of Greeks wanting to see Him?

_____

_____

In what way did Jesus say He—the Son of Man—would be glorified?

- If a single seed dies and is buried, "it produces many seeds" (John 12:23-26).

  _____

  _____

- If the Son of Man is "lifted up from the earth," He will draw all to Himself (John 12:28-33).

  _____

  _____

The glory of the fig tree is not its leafy foliage but the fruit that leaves the tree. The glory of the Temple was not its magnificence or lavish rituals but those who left healed and forgiven. The glory of Jesus was not in remaining to perform "miraculous signs in their presence" but in being lifted up on the cross, that those who look will see and believe in *the One who sent Him*—a light drawing all to eternal life.

FRUITFULNESS—A VIRAL MOVEMENT PRINCIPLE

In *Fruitful Church: A Manifesto for Sending*, Andrew Turner argues that "numbers are important, especially when the numbers represent people who are precious to God"—but churches are notorious for counting the wrong people. Turner continues, "We should measure success not by the number of people that come in to our church, but by the number and calibre of believers who are sent out from it."[4] He adds, "We raise our children to mature, leave home, and start new households. Why is this the norm for families, but the exception for churches?"[5] Consider the following:

- Jesus chose the twelve, calling them "sent ones" (Mark 3:13-15).
- Andrew Turner writes, "Fruit, by definition, leaves the tree. . . . Fruit carries seed for multiplication."[6]
- If a single seed "dies, it produces many seeds" (John 12:24).

REFLECTION

How might a culture of retention, rather than sending, be negative for a movement?

_____

_____

Why must movement leaders die for disciple-making movements to go viral?

_____

_____

What might Jesus have meant when He said, "Streams of living water will flow from within" believers (John 7:37-39)?

_____

_____

What could dying—leaving, getting out of the way—for fruitfulness mean for you?

_____

_____

SHARING

Discuss with your friends: What if we equipped our young people to leave church by age sixteen to eighteen to plant the next generation of groups or churches?

_____

_____

What can you share with those you are leading to Jesus?

_____

_____

LOVE

The Most Important Command

JESUS SPENT THE NIGHTS of this final week on the Mount of Olives, returning early to the Temple each morning. On His last day of "preaching the gospel" (Luke 20:1) in the Temple courts, He was pursued by chief priests, Pharisees, Sadducees, and Herodians. Teachers and experts in law challenged, set traps, interrogated, and quizzed him. It was intense. They were out to get Him! Within three days, He would be crucified. What vital viral movement principle did He emphasize?

READ

- Matthew 21:23–23:39; Mark 11:27–12:44; Luke 20:1–21:4
- *Messiah*, chapters 66–67

What do you think of Jesus' response to the demand of the officials—"Who gave you this authority" to do what you are doing (Matthew 21:23-27)?

_____

_____

Jesus responded further with three parables. What was He highlighting?

- The two sons asked to work in their father's vineyard
  (Matthew 21:28-32).

  _____

  _____

- The tenants who killed the landowner's son (Matthew 21:33-46).

  _____

  _____

- The guests invited by the king to the wedding banquet
  (Matthew 22:1-14).

  _____

  _____

AVOIDING THE TRAPS

Imagine how much Jesus infuriated the Temple leaders. He said tax collectors and prostitutes were entering the Kingdom ahead of them, and then He labeled them ungrateful murderers who contrived to enter the Kingdom on their own terms. So they "laid plans to trap him."

Pharisees colluded with the Herodians, supporters of Herod Antipas, to present a politically charged question. What was the trap (Matthew 22:15-22)?

_____

_____

Sadducees, who didn't believe in the Resurrection, came with a puzzling question. How did Jesus expose their disregard for Scripture (Matthew 22:23-33)?

_____

_____

A Pharisee posed a legal question: "Which is the greatest commandment in the Law?" Reflect on the depth of Jesus' insight (Matthew 22:34-40; Mark 12:28-34).

_____

_____

LOVE GOD—LOVE OTHERS

Having identified these two great commands, Jesus took the initiative to expose His accuser's lack of love for God or others.

What was the attitude of Pharisees to the Messiah, the Lord (Matthew 22:41-46)?

_____

_____

What cynical attitude toward others did their actions display (Matthew 23:1-12)?

_____

_____

Jesus was uncompromising. His movement was founded on radical, counterintuitive principles, evident in attitudes and actions. "The greatest among you will be your servant," He said. "For whoever exalts himself will be humbled, and whoever humbles himself will be exalted" (Matthew 23:11-12).

HYPOCRISY AND HUMILITY

Jesus leveled the most scathing rebukes at the teachers of the law and Pharisees. He likened them to actors who wore masks. In the theater, the *hypocrite* put on a face for dramatic entertainment, but the deception of these religious leaders was no play. Seven times He declared, "Woe to you . . ."—six times addressing them as *hypocrites* and once as "blind guides."

What was under the mask? Why was their deception so evil (Matthew 23:13-36)?

_____

_____

Why did Jesus express such deep sorrow over Jerusalem? In what condition had deception left the Temple and people (Matthew 23:37-39)?

_____

_____

Then, sitting near where offerings were brought to the Temple treasury, Jesus saw a widow give "two very small copper coins." For this woman, life had been stripped away. She had lost her husband, her support. She had no stage, no mask! The contrast was stark. What did Jesus want His disciples to understand (Mark 12:41-44; Luke 21:1-4)?

_____

_____

LOVE—A VIRAL MOVEMENT PRINCIPLE

In *Movements that Change the World*, Steve Addison identifies five prerequisites for movements. The first is *white-hot faith*.[1] It is passionate, genuine, transparent, courageous love for God and others that ignites *white-hot faith*.

Jesus identified two great commands: "Love the Lord your God with all your heart and with all your soul and with all your mind and with all your strength" and "Love your neighbor as yourself." He said, "There is no commandment greater than these"—and all others "hang on these" (Matthew 22:37-40; Mark 12:29-31).

How did this principle define early believers (Acts 2:42-47; 4:32-37)?

_____

_____

What practical actions flow from love, making it such a fundamental principle for viral movements?

_____

_____

SHARING

Discuss with your friends how to address hypocrisy in your life or movement.

_____

_____

Why do you think Jesus' rebuke of hypocrites, together with His affirmation of the widow, might appeal to those you are leading to Him?

_____

_____

FAITHFULNESS

Watching and Working

JESUS HAD TAUGHT for the last time in the Temple courts. "You will not see me again," He said, "until you say, 'Blessed is he who comes in the name of the Lord'" (Matthew 23:39). But He had not finished for the day. As He left for the Mount of Olives, His disciples drew attention to the glory of the Temple: "What massive stones! What magnificent buildings!" His response was confronting. "Do you see all these great buildings?" he asked. "Not one stone here will be left on another; every one will be thrown down" (Mark 13:1-2).

Crossing the Kidron Valley, they sat on the Mount of Olives. The Temple was in full view, its golden facades glowing in the evening light. Alone with Jesus, the disciples had opportunity to ask, "When will this [destruction] happen and what will be the sign of your coming and of the end of the age?" (Matthew 24:3). Jesus' response, followed by five parables specifically for His movement leaders, urged them to remain faithful, to watch, and to work. He warned of threats to His Kingdom movement.

READ
- Matthew 24:1–25:46; Mark 13:1-37; Luke 21:5-36
- *Messiah*, chapters 69–70

KEEP WATCHING

Three times Jesus warned of deception. What were His concerns?

- Matthew 24:4-8:

_____

_____

- Matthew 24:9-14:

_____

_____

- Matthew 24:15-28:

_____

_____

The devastation Jesus prophesied alarmed His disciples. If such turmoil engulfed Jerusalem in the end times, how would they recognize Him? What would be the sign of His coming?[1] Scanning the horizon of the future, Jesus foretold the siege and destruction of Jerusalem by the Romans in AD 70—and looked further to His glorious return.

"When you see Jerusalem being surrounded by armies," Jesus had warned, "you will know that its desolation is near. Then let those who are in Judea flee to the mountains, let those in the city get out, and let those in the country not enter the city" (Luke 21:20-21). They were not to resist, just flee!

Their opportunity came when Cestius withdrew from Jerusalem, giving time for those who remembered Jesus' words to flee from the city and cross the Jordan to Pela in Perea,[2] before General Titus returned to utterly devastate the city and Temple.

Jesus' promise of His glorious return is as certain as His predictions of Jerusalem's destruction.

But the disciples wanted to know how they would recognize Him. What would be the sign that it was Him (Matthew 24:29-31)?

_____

_____

What point was Jesus concerned to get across (Matthew 24:32-41)?

_____

_____

KEEP WATCHING, AND KEEP WORKING

Jesus did not want His movement leaders to miss what He was saying. He shared six parables to underscore His point: "Therefore keep watch, because you do not know on what day your Lord will come" (Matthew 24:42).

What key ideas did He repeat? Together with watching, what point is Jesus making in each of these stories?

- The homeowner and his servants (Mark 13:33-37)

  _____

  _____

- The homeowner and the thief (Matthew 24:43-44)

  _____

  _____

- The faithful and wise servant (Matthew 24:45-51)

  _____

  _____

- The ten virgins waiting for the bridegroom (Matthew 25:1-13)

  _____

  _____

- The businessman entrusting his property to his servants (Matthew 25:14-30)

  _____

  _____

- The sheep and the goats (Matthew 25:31-46)

  _____

  _____

KEEP WORKING

On His first ministry visit to Jerusalem, Jesus declared He was the one-man temple—before going out to heal and forgive, taking the work of the Temple to rich and poor, Jew and Gentile.

Now, on this Tuesday afternoon, leaving the Temple for the last time, Jesus said, "Your house is left to you desolate. . . . You will not see me again until you say, 'Blessed is he that comes in the name of the Lord'" (Matthew 23:38-39).

That evening, seated on the Mount of Olives with His movement leaders, He emphasized that His followers were to continue His Temple work of healing and forgiving. Again He spoke of judgment, tying eternal destiny to the treatment of "the least of these brothers of mine" (Matthew 25:40).

It is a stark, breathtaking picture: the Son of Man on a heavenly throne surrounded by angels, rendering His verdict of "eternal punishment" or "eternal life" (Matthew 25:46). Who might "these brothers of mine" be (Matthew 25:34-40)?[3]

Could they be the disciples?

In Matthew's Gospel, Jesus' disciples were His *brothers* (Matthew 12:48-50, 28:10). He sent out the Twelve (Matthew 10:1-42) without money, food, drink, clothing, or homes—and with the threat of arrest—saying: "He who receives you receives me, and he who receives me receives the one who sent me" (Matthew 10:40).

_____

_____

Could they be the marginalized, the poor, and the needy?

In Matthew 10 and 25, faith and justice are linked, and the rewards are similar: "And if anyone gives even a cup of cold water to one of these little ones because he is my disciple, I tell you the truth, he will certainly not lose his reward" (Matthew 10:42; compare 25:40). Salvation is dependent on one's response to gospel proclamation.[4]

_____

_____

WATCHING AND WORKING—A VIRAL MOVEMENT PRINCIPLE

We are not to be impressed with grand buildings. Herod's temple was massive and magnificent, overlaid with gold—but it would disappear. The ceremonies and rituals were dramatic and captivating—but they would pass. We are not to be consumed by wars, rumors of conflict, dark days, blood moons, or star showers. Jesus told His movement leaders to be observant but not distracted from their mission of disciplemaking. They were to keep watching and keep working!

What is to be accomplished in the midst of ongoing turmoil (Matthew 24:14)?

_____

_____

What quality does Jesus affirm (Matthew 25:21, 23)?

_____

_____

How does the Judgment demonstrate the upside-down status reversal of His Kingdom (Matthew 25:31-46)?

_____

_____

SHARING

Discuss with friends the significance of faithfulness in watching and working in Jesus' Kingdom movement.

_____

_____

What can you share with those you are encouraging to be disciples of Jesus?

_____

_____

THE DISINHERITED

"What She Has Done Will Be Told"

FOLLOWING THE CONFRONTATION, prophecies, and teaching of Tuesday, the Wednesday of Jesus' last week was a quiet day. If we follow the placement of events as recorded by Matthew and Mark, the only recorded event was an invitation to a meal in Bethany.[1]

Each evening of this final week, Jesus found refuge on the Mount of Olives or in this village. Over the ridge and out of sight, this was an ideal settlement for the *disinherited*, including lepers and others banned from the city and Temple areas.[2] The Temple leaders wanted to be rid of Jesus but, in Bethany, He was among friends, and the meal was held in his honor. What insight did Jesus have for His movement leaders?

READ
- Matthew 26:1-16; Mark 14:1-11; Luke 22:1-6; John 12:2-8
- *Messiah*, chapter 62

A LEPER
Some believe Simon the Pharisee (Luke 7:36-50) was also this Simon the leper, reconciling the stories as reports by different witnesses. As mentioned previously, in these guides, we treat them as different, the first living in Galilee, the other in Bethany.[3]

Reflect on the stark contrast between the gatherings that evening: one at the palace of the High Priest Caiaphas in Jerusalem, the other in the home of Simon the leper in Bethany. What motivated each gathering (Matthew 26:1-6; John 12:2)?

A WOMAN

Simon was not the only outcast. Women were also disinherited. Other rabbis called only male disciples, but without shame, Jesus invited and welcomed women as disciples. They were integral to His movement, many traveling with Him (Luke 8:1-3, see also Luke 23:55 and Acts 1:14).

Mary—sister of Martha and Lazarus—was a disciple. She sat with the men, and Jesus would not take this away from her (Luke 10:42). Her testimony—"You are the Christ, the Son of God" (John 11:27)—matched Peter's.[4] Now, just before Passover, what was her intent (Matthew 26:6-13)?

In medieval times, it was assumed this Mary was the same as Mary Magdalene, but Mary was a popular female name among Jews, used fifty-one times in the New Testament. With no direct connection in Scripture, we cannot necessarily assume they are the same.[5]

Mary went to Simon's home—into the company of men, including her brother—bringing the most expensive perfume. Jesus had foretold His crucifixion, but His male disciples had dismissed His predictions. What indicates that Mary understood what Jesus was saying?[6]

By His response, what did Jesus make clear?

A BETRAYER IN THEIR MIDST

If Judas Iscariot was from the village of Kriyot on the border of Judea—as his name indicates[7]—he was the only non-Galilean among the Twelve.

Gradually, he realized Jesus had no intention of fulfilling triumphal expectations of the Messiah. Jesus had again spoken of His burial. Judas determined to "goad him into resistance."[8]

It seems Judas hurried back into Jerusalem to find the religious authorities gathered, plotting to kill Jesus. While he expressed dismay that the money spent by Mary was not given for the poor, what scheme did he devise (Matthew 26:8-16; compare John 12:4-6)?

_____

_____

THE DISINHERITED

Judas Iscariot and others were indignant—what a waste! But Jesus responded, "She has done a beautiful thing to me," preparing for His burial (Matthew 26:10-12). Then He declared, "I tell you the truth, wherever this gospel is preached throughout the world, what she has done will also be told, in memory of her" (Matthew 26:13). In effect, Jesus was saying that when you remember Him, you will remember her![9]

Jesus lived in a shame–honor society in which women were the possession of men, in which the weak and vulnerable—the poor, disabled, sick, demon-possessed, children, youth, refugees, and foreigners—were considered unclean and unlovely. They were banned to the fringes, *disinherited* by society and religion.

Consider how Jesus affirmed the disinherited that He met in His last week:

- lepers (Simon)

_____

_____

- women (Mary)

_____

_____

- poor (Mark 12:41-44; Luke 21:1-4—the poor widow)

_____

_____

- disabled (Matthew 21:14)

_____

_____

- children and youth (Matthew 21:15-16)

_____

_____

- foreigners (John 12:20-26)

_____

_____

Jesus had a high regard for the *disinherited*. They were integral to His Kingdom of status-reversal. He welcomed them. He—the Suffering Servant (Isaiah 52:13–56:8)—had come to bring honor, dignity, and salvation for them—the afflicted, foreigners, and eunuchs, including those "born that way" (Isaiah 56:1-8; compare Matthew 19:12).

Who might be the disinherited today?

_____

_____

ENGAGING THE DISINHERITED—A VIRAL MOVEMENT PRINCIPLE

For Jesus, the *disinherited* are Kingdom people, key to His disciple-making movement. In *The Social Sources of Denominationalism*, Richard Niebuhr gave detailed attention to the birth of new churches by the *disinherited*, concluding that they are the ones who cultivate movements.[10]

Breaking the flask, Mary poured the perfume on Jesus' head and feet, wiping His feet with her hair. The room was filled with the fragrance, the catalyst that drove Judas to conspire with religious authorities to destroy Jesus' disciple-making movement.

Why might denominational and institutional church systems often sabotage the full participation of youth, women, those less affluent or "successful," those who are different?

_____

_____

How does your movement proactively encourage initiatives by the disinherited?

_____

_____

REFLECTION

What fresh (even novel) insights have you gained from this guide?

_____

_____

In your context, who are the disinherited?

_____

_____

SHARING

Discuss with your friends the significance of the disinherited to a viral movement.

_____

_____

What can you share with those you are encouraging to be disciples of Jesus?

_____

_____

SUBVERSIVE HUMILITY

On the Path of Life

"IT WAS JUST before the Passover Feast. Jesus knew that *the time had come* for him to leave this world and go to the Father" (John 13:1, emphasis added). He would spend one last day with His movement leaders, then everything would change. This Passover would be like no other. His disciples had no comprehension of how dramatically their hopes and aspirations would be dashed. Before the end of Passover, Jesus would be dead. In a short time, there was much for them to learn.

READ
- Matthew 26:17-35; Mark 14:12-31; Luke 22:7-38; John 13:1-38
- *Messiah*, chapters 71–72

PREPARATION FOR THE LAST SUPPER

Preparation was to be made on Thursday, the fourteenth day of the month of Nissan, for the Passover supper that evening. Lambs were sacrificed in the afternoon[1] and prepared, with the women cooking complementary dishes and decorating the room.

What is fascinating about Jesus' directions for finding a suitable room (Mark 14:12-16)?

Unless he was an Essene, it was unusual for a man to be carrying a water jar in the city.[2] This was the work of women. Jesus was aware of an ongoing dispute among His disciples over status, over "which of them was considered to be greatest" (Luke 22:24). Might His choice of water carrier have challenged their expectations of status? When they met in the upper room that evening, how did Jesus demonstrate "the full extent of his love" for them (John 13:1)—and further challenge their hierarchical-status models of Kingdom?

Jesus took the role of a slave. (John 13:1-20)

Washing feet was a daily activity for slaves. Jesus "humbled himself," "made himself nothing, taking the very nature of a servant [slave]" (Philippians 2:7-8). Such humility was radically countercultural. Some call it cruciform,[3] the attitude of self-denial that led Jesus to die for others. Jesus' example must not be limited to one daily task nor a ceremony of *foot washing* practiced intermittently, sometimes called the Ordinance of Humility.[4] He set an example of status reversal.

How could such radical, countercultural, subversive humility pervade the lives of disciplemakers today?

Jesus rejected the system of benefactors. (Luke 22:24-30)

Jesus subverted the accepted "social pyramid." Mark Strom observes that demarcations of rank—free, freed, or slave—"stamped a person for life."[5] Benefactors or patrons were the *free* or *freed*. Work was beneath them. They spent their time manipulating from the top, giving for city works or the poor—but always seeking to impress, to gain support, prestige, influence, and dependence from others. There were *no free lunches*; those they helped always *owed them*. Whether slave or freed, all were bound to their patron or benefactor. In a similar way, the priests of the Temple made people dependent on them.

What are practical implications of Jesus' clear message that patronage is never to be the way of His Kingdom or His movement leaders?

_____

_____

DISTRESS—BETRAYAL AND DENIAL

After Jesus had served as a slave, He dressed and returned to the table. Reclining nearest Him, John noticed He was "troubled in spirit." Then Jesus said, "I tell you the truth, one of you is going to betray me" (John 13:21).

Judas sat at a place of honor next to Jesus. What indicates Judas might have assumed the role of benefactor, therefore being embarrassed by Jesus doing slave work and stung by the idea that a master was to be a servant (John 13:21-30)?

_____

_____

Once Judas had left the room, Jesus spoke of being glorified. How do you understand this in the context of betrayal, "falling away," and denial (John 13:31-38; compare Matthew 26:31-35)?

_____

_____

FAITH ON THE PATH OF LIFE

While eating the Passover meal—the memorial of deliverance from captivity in Egypt—Jesus instituted a simple, symbolic meal as a reminder of salvation from slavery to sin. This meal played a major part in His movement going viral, for it placed His message on the path of everyday life for all people. He took from the table two items common to most household meals, bread and drink.[6] He blessed them, saying, "Whenever you eat this bread and drink this cup, you *proclaim* the Lord's death until he comes" (1 Corinthians 11:26, emphasis added).

Reflect on how this simple meal became a daily declaration of the gospel:

- Matthew 26:26-29; Mark 14:22-25; Luke 22:17-20:

  _____

  _____

- Acts 2:42-47:

  _____

  _____

- 1 Corinthians 11:23-26:

  _____

  _____

As disciples multiplied across the empire, the message of Jesus Christ was repeated and proclaimed every day, at each household meal. Effectively, "the cross of Calvary [was] stamped on every loaf of bread."[7] Whenever a family gathered, the father blessed their bread and drink, proclaiming: "This is a symbol of our Lord and Savior Jesus Christ, crucified, risen, seated at the right hand of the Father, and coming again."[8]

With Roman emperors honored as lord and savior, in what way was the Lord's Supper a revolutionary declaration?

_____

_____

SUBVERSIVE HUMILITY ON THE PATHS OF LIFE— A VIRAL MOVEMENT PRINCIPLE

There are two aspects to this principle:

1. *Subversive humility:* Humility was not a quality valued by the powerful. Rank and status defined society. When pregnant with Jesus, His mother's song reflected aspirations for freedom from oppression:[9] "He has brought down rulers from their thrones *but has lifted up the humble*" (Luke 1:52, emphasis added). Jesus did that!

2. *Everyday activities:* Jesus chose simple, humble, everyday activities (such as washing feet and eating) as practical, regular, and revolutionary statements of faith in Him.

In what way did Jesus' new command epitomize His radical message of subversive humility (John 13:34-35)?

_____

_____

Rather than accommodating culture, what might be the impact of countercultural faith?

_____

_____

REFLECTION

What has been new in this guide?

_____

_____

What is humility? How does humility honor the other person as of the greatest value?

_____

_____

SHARING

Discuss with your friends: What everyday activities might be reclaimed or redefined as declarations of faith in your movement of disciplemaking?

_____

_____

What can you share with those you are encouraging to be disciples of Jesus?

_____

_____

SUCCESSION TO HOLY SPIRIT PRESENCE

ALTHOUGH JESUS ALSO SPOKE of resurrection (Matthew 26:32; Mark 14:28), His ominous predictions of betrayal, denial, and death filled His disciples with dread. Would His movement fail? Was this the end? What would happen to them? They had invested a lot in following Jesus!

As their leader, Jesus had brought His disciples to a critical point. For His movement to go viral, it was time for Him to leave. This is a point at which many movements fail. Unlike John the Baptist, Barnabas, and Paul, many leaders wish to hang on, to be in control. But Jesus had a succession plan, one that would prove "utterly magnetic for an empire overrun by slavery, abuse of women and minorities, debauched sexuality, oppression, and injustice."[1]

READ
- John 14:1–18:12; Matthew 26:30-56; Mark 14:26-52; Luke 22:39-53
- *Messiah*, chapter 73–74

THEIR ONGOING ASSIGNMENT

Jesus had revealed the Father. He was now about to leave. What were the disciples to do (John 14:1-14)?

_____

_____

THEIR NEW RELATIONSHIP WITH JESUS

Jesus would ask the Father to send the Holy Spirit, who had filled His life. How would their relationship with Jesus change (John 14:15-31)?

Reflect on Jesus' statement: "I will not leave you as orphans; I will come to you. Before long, the world will not see me anymore, but you will see me. Because I live, you also will live. On that day you will realize that I am in my Father, and you are in me, and I am in you" (John 14:18-20).

What would be their new relationship with Jesus and His Father through the Holy Spirit's presence (John 14:23)?

_____

_____

In what way was this closer than any prior experience with Jesus?

_____

_____

If this is possible for all disciples, what is our privilege?

_____

_____

Their relationship to Jesus had changed. They were no longer servants but friends. What were the implications for the disciples as movement leaders (John 15:1-17)?

_____

_____

Their friendship with Jesus would result in expulsion from the synagogue—a center of social life for Jewish men—and even death. What would motivate them in the face of such persecution (John 15:18–16:4)?

_____

_____

When Jesus spoke of His imminent death, what significant foundational
principle did He lay for His movement to go viral (John 16:5-33)?

_____

_____

TRANSITION TIME HAD COME

Special times of prayer preceded several major transitions in Jesus' disciple-making and movement building. Following His baptism, as He moved from the *preparation* years to His *ministry foundations* phase, He prayed beside the Jordan. Then, with disciples multiplying, and facing threats from Herodians and Pharisees, Jesus spent the night in prayer before selecting His twelve movement leaders. The time had now come for Him to be glorified and to hand His movement to His Holy Spirit-anointed disciples. It was His time of sacrifice—and prayer!

There were two times of prayer:

- Three intercessory prayers as they left the upper room for Gethsemane.

    What was His prayer for Himself, His disciples, and His future
    movement as He prepared for His departure (John 17:1-26)?

    _____

    _____

- Three agonizing prayers in Gethsemane.

    In His darkest hour, with the weight of the world's sin upon Him,
    what resolution did Jesus make (John 18:1; Matthew 26:30-46;
    Mark 14:26-42; Luke 22:39-46)?

    _____

    _____

BETRAYAL AND DESERTION

Judas guided "a detachment of [up to six hundred] soldiers,"[2] together with temple officials and "a large crowd armed with swords and clubs," into the grove. If it wasn't so tragic, it would be comical. Everything was *over the top*: Judas's kiss of betrayal when Jesus had already identified Himself; Peter's inept use of his sword, removing the ear of the high priest's servant, when Jesus could have called for "twelve legions of angels"; the binding of Jesus, when He could have been taken during daylight hours, as He taught in the Temple courts. Mark records: "Then *everyone* deserted him and fled," including one young man—whom tradition identifies as John Mark—escaping naked!

Amid the confusion, what indicates Jesus knew His movement was on track (Matthew 26:47-56; Mark 14:43-52; Luke 22:47-53; John 18:2-12)?

SUCCESSION TO HOLY SPIRIT PRESENCE—A VIRAL MOVEMENT PRINCIPLE

Politicians sometimes outlive their popularity, with no succession plan. Unable to manipulate the constitution, some turn dictator. Some corporate directors use the courts to maintain control. At times, denominational executives lobby to hold office. These are not the responses of movement leaders. Movement leaders equip others and move on. What do we learn from New Testament leaders about this viral movement principle?

In the following examples, the movement leader was removed violently:

- John the Baptist—prepared the way for Jesus and was then imprisoned (Matthew 4:12; 14:1-12)

- Paul—completed his third missionary journey and was then imprisoned (Acts 21:1–23:35)

Barnabas encouraged the early church movement and then went to Cyprus and disappeared from records (Acts 15:36-41).

Why is succession planning for leaders an essential viral movement principle? Why is it often not done?

_____

_____

But Jesus' succession plan was more comprehensive. He was not handing over His mission to the narrow restraint of a few selected, ordained leaders.[3] *Every believer would be Holy Spirit–filled. What are the implications of this for multiplying disciple-making movements today?*

_____

_____

SHARING

What restraints do we place on the principle of involving every believer?

_____

_____

What can you share with those you are encouraging to be disciples of Jesus?

_____

_____

SACRIFICE FOR OTHERS

"Greater Love Has No One Than This"

IN A KIDRON VALLEY olive grove, east of the Temple Mount and city wall, was Gethsemane: an oil press. There, anticipating the extreme emotional and physical horror of separation from His Father, Jesus' body began to break down—sweating blood! Clinical studies have shown that "blood sweat," a very rare condition, might be accompanied by excruciating headaches and abdominal pain.[1] But Jesus' focus was clear: "Greater love has no one than this, that he lay down his life for his friends" (John 15:13).

From Gethsemane, the mob moved quickly. There were three phases to the Jewish trial, followed by three to the Roman trial, and Jesus was on the cross by nine o'clock the next morning! How could such an end be the foundation of His Kingdom movement? From these dark hours, what did Jesus' movement leaders learn?

READ
- Matthew 26:57–27:56; Mark 14:53–15:41; Luke 22:54–23:49; John 18:13–19:30
- *Messiah*, chapters 75–79

JESUS DID NOT STAND UP

Expectations of a strong, military Messiah were turned upside down. Bound, He weakly submitted to horrendous abuse, as He was slapped, punched, beaten, mocked, and spat on.

In the three Jewish phases of trial—before Annas, Caiaphas, and the Sanhedrin—Jesus only answered one question. The high priest asked, "Tell us if you are the Christ, the Son of God." How did Jesus respond, and what clarification did He make (Matthew 26:63-64)?

_____

_____

Peter "followed him at a distance." Early in the morning, drawn into the courtyard of the high priest, he was questioned about his association with Jesus. Why do you think he responded with such aggressive denials (Matthew 26:69-75)?

_____

_____

At daybreak, with Jesus before them, an assembly of "the chief priests, with the elders, the teachers of the law and the whole Sanhedrin" reached the decision "to put Jesus to death" (Matthew 27:1; Mark 15:1). Why such drastic action from Judas (Matthew 27:3-10)?

_____

_____

JESUS CLARIFIED THE CHARGE

Again, in the three phases of his Roman trials—before Pilate, the Roman governor of Jerusalem, Herod Antipas of Galilee, and back before Pilate[2]—Jesus answered only one question. Pilate asked, "Are you the king of the Jews?" How did Jesus respond, and what clarification did He give (Matthew 27:11-14; John 18:33-38)?

_____

_____

It was clear to Pilate that he was not dealing with a criminal. False witnesses in the Jewish trial had failed to find Jesus guilty of crime. To Pilate's amazement, Jesus refused to engage with the Jew's fallacious accusations, and before Herod Antipas, He remained silent, refusing to humor with miracles. Pilate declared, "I find no basis for a charge against this man" and "neither has Herod" (Luke 23:4, 14-15; John 18:38).

But despite Jesus' innocence, Pilate sat in the judge's seat, attempting to strike a deal with the leaders and crowd. A disturbing message from his wife urged caution. How did Pilate's attempt to use the murderous political rebel Barabbas as a bargaining chip for Jesus' release further clarify who Jesus really was (Matthew 27:15-26)?

VIA DOLOROSA—HIS JOURNEY OF PAIN

Jesus' refusal to answer His accusers or Pilate's questions frustrated the governor. "Don't you realize I have power either to free you or to crucify you?" he demanded. Jesus answered, "You would have no power over me if it were not given to you from above" (John 19:10-11).

"With one voice" the chief priests, rulers and crowd were baying for blood: "Away with this man! Release Barabbas to us!" (Luke 23:18). The chief priests declared, "We have no king but Caesar" (John 19:15).

Pilate had Jesus flogged and crowned with thorns, but the temple officials were not satisfied. "Crucify him! Crucify him!" they shouted. The third time Pilate asked, "Why? What crime has this man committed? I have found in him no grounds for the death penalty." But, when he saw he was "getting nowhere" and "wanting to satisfy the crowd," Pilate released Barabbas, "washed his hands" of Jesus, and "handed him over to be crucified" (Luke 23:22; Matthew 27:24; Mark 15:15).

Imagine all involved: Pilate's soldiers, Simon of Cyrene (and maybe his boys), and the two criminals being led with Jesus to execution. What might Jesus' comment to the crowds—"including women who mourned and wailed for him"—have meant to each (Luke 23:27-31; compare Matthew 27:27-34; Mark 15:16-23; John 19:16-17)?

CRUCIFIXION

Jesus was taken outside the city to a roadside site called Golgotha, the Skull. No details are given about His crucifixion, but first-century citizens understood it fully. The memories were too shocking, painful. This was Rome's "most insidious and intimidating instrument of power and political control," the most miserable, torturous, violent, shameful death possible.[3] For Jews, it was God's curse (Deuteronomy 21:23). The Gospel writers simply record that "they crucified him" (Matthew 27:35; Mark 15:24; Luke 23:33; John 19:18).

Pilate had a notice placed on the cross: "Jesus of Nazareth, the king of the Jews" (John 19:19-20). Why in three languages? Why was this so offensive to the chief priests?

_____

_____

Naked, abused, covered with blood and filth, His ankles nailed to the upright, His hands and arms tied and nailed to the crossbeam, Jesus was at eye level with those around Him. Despite the agony, in the first three hours, Jesus reached out to those near Him.

The paradox could not be more obvious. Jesus was being torn apart, yet the soldiers say, "Let's not tear [his garment]." What was Jesus' response (Luke 23:34)?

_____

_____

While insults were being hurled about His inability to save, what assurance did Jesus give the repentant thief (Luke 23:35-43)?

_____

_____

Then Jesus saw His mother. She and John must have been nearby, for Him to talk with them. Reflect on His care for her (John 19:25-27).

_____

_____

At noon, the sky became dark as night. Jesus' fourth statement—of His seven statements from the cross—came right after the sky turned black:

"My God, my God, why have you forsaken me?" (Matthew 27:46). Jesus was quoting Psalm 22. The apostle Paul understood: "God made him who had no sin to be sin for us, so that in him we might become the righteousness of God" (2 Corinthians 5:21).

In what way did this awful experience, anticipated by Jesus in Gethsemane, reveal the inner life of our triune God?

_____

_____

Exhausted, Jesus said, "I am thirsty." Jesus' humanity was fully revealed—even exposed—in His last moments of life. In what ways is this important to you as a follower of Jesus (John 19:28-30)?

_____

_____

Jesus cried out, "Father, into your hands I commit my spirit" (Luke 23:46). In what way did His surrender of His spirit—Holy Spirit or life[4]—demonstrate total trust?

_____

_____

What dramatic events accompanied His final declaration, "It is finished" (John 19:30; see Matthew 27:51-56; Mark 15:38-41; Luke 23:45-49)?

_____

_____

SACRIFICE FOR OTHERS—A VIRAL MOVEMENT PRINCIPLE

By 3:00 p.m., Jesus was dead. His crucifixion now defines our view of God:[5] a "working man,"[6] a "blue-collar messiah,"[7] killed as a slave between two thieves, cruciform.[8]

Amid extreme suffering, how did Jesus relate to others?

- His tormentors:

_____

_____

- His fellow condemned:

  _____

  _____

- His family:

  _____

  _____

- His disciples and movement leaders:

  _____

  _____

What might Jesus' movement leaders have learned from His hours of suffering and sacrifice for others?

_____

_____

In what way did Jesus' sacrifice redefine divine power and glory?

_____

_____

REFLECTION

In reflecting on Jesus' sacrifice, what fresh insight have you gained?

_____

_____

How could a cruciform attitude redefine our relationships with others?

_____

_____

SHARING

Discuss with your friends how sacrifice for others is the foundation to a viral movement.

_____

_____

What can you share with those you are encouraging to be disciples of Jesus?

_____

_____

PASSIONATE WITNESS TO THE GOOD NEWS

JESUS' WAY IS COUNTERINTUITIVE. While perfection, performance, and power appeal, Jesus suffered to win and died to give life. By His crucifixion Jesus revealed the inner life of God, mutual subordination for the other, as the foundation of His disciple-making movement. Nothing could reveal God's passionate love for us more than His taking our sin upon Himself, enduring the separation and death that sin brings.

By midday that Friday, darkness enveloped the land; by midafternoon, the Temple was devastated, a violent earthquake wrenched rocks apart, and Jesus was dead.

The agony since His Gethsemane prayer had gone unanswered, the "appalling silence of the Father," "the experience of hell and judgment" when God withdrew[1]—all culminated in Jesus' cry, "My God, my God. Why have you exposed me to shame? Why have you cursed me? It is finished!"[2]

READ

- Matthew 27:45–28:20; Mark 15:33–16:18; Luke 23:44–24:49; John 19:28–21:25
- *Messiah*, chapters 80–86

WITNESSES TO JESUS' DEATH

What do you understand as the meaning of the dramatic events that followed Jesus' cry (Matthew 27:45-53; Mark 15:33-38; Luke 23:44-46; John 19:28-30)?

_____

_____

"This cry of God's forsaken Son stands at the centre of Christian faith," writes Jürgen Moltmann. It is the only time Jesus did not call God "my Father." Far from, and without God, Jesus tasted death for all (Hebrews 2:9).[3] How did witnesses react (Matthew 27:54-56; Mark 15:39-41; Luke 23:47-49)?

_____

_____

The moment Jesus died, the massive curtain veiling access to the Most Holy Place of the Temple was torn from top to bottom. With the Son separated from Father and Spirit, God's triune fellowship was shattered. Creation shook, "rocks split," and, the author of Hebrews declares, Jesus tore open "a new and living way" for us to enter the Most Holy and "draw near to God"—"through the curtain, that is his body" (Hebrews 10:19-22).

_____

_____

CERTIFICATION OF DEATH

How certain were Jewish authorities, Roman soldiers, Joseph of Arimathea (a member of the Jewish Council), Nicodemus, and Jesus' disciples—including "many women"—that Jesus was dead (Matthew 27:57-66; Mark 15:42-47; Luke 23:50-56; John 19:31-42)?

_____

_____

THE TOMB

While the Church of the Holy Sepulchre in Jerusalem is inside today's Old City walls, this site was outside the city in Jesus' time. Up the stairs and behind glass is bedrock, perhaps the remains of the location of Golgotha, where Jesus was crucified. In AD 135, Hadrian built a pagan temple at the site. But, in AD 326, workmen looking for the tomb of Jesus believed they found it, and it remains as a small chapel. With first-century graves present, it is a possible location for Jesus' death and burial.

Then, in the nineteenth century, the site of the Garden Tomb, north of the Damascus Gate, was suggested as an alternative site of Calvary and Jesus' tomb. This tomb is too ancient to have been new in the time of Joseph of Arimathea, but the garden, cistern, winepress, and tomb provide a much more realistic and inspiring setting for reflection today.[4]

CREATION AND SALVATION

"In the beginning," after six days, with His work of Creation complete, Jesus rested on *the seventh day*—and there was a garden there (Genesis 1:1; 2:1-3). Then, on Passover Friday, the "blood of the new covenant" was shed. His life "ended so disgracefully that nothing worse was humanly imaginable."[5] On a tree, under God's curse (Deuteronomy 21:23), His agonizing cry of total separation came from the first verse of Psalm 22: "My God, my God, why have you forsaken me?" His final words reflected the last verse: "He has done it" (Psalm 22:1, 31). And, having completed all work necessary for the salvation and reconciliation of His creation, Jesus again rested on *the Sabbath*—in a garden (John 19:41-42).

Jesus rested, as did His female disciples (Luke 23:55-56), but the Temple authorities were uneasy. While the disciples failed to grasp Jesus' prophecies about His resurrection, the chief priests and Pharisees recalled what He had said (Matthew 12:40, 16:4; John 2:19-20)[6]—and they were prepared to break the Sabbath to achieve their ends. How did they propose to secure the tomb against Jesus' resurrection (Matthew 27:62-66)?

WITNESSES TO JESUS' RESURRECTION

No one actually saw Jesus rise from the grave or walk from the tomb. After Shabbat, early Sunday morning, women were the first to the tomb.

*What evidence did they—and Peter and John—find that Jesus had risen?
What might your reaction have been (Matthew 28:1-8; Mark 16:1-8;
Luke 24:1-12; John 20:1-10)?*

This was not a *near-death experience*, an apparition, or a reincarnation.
Nor was Jesus simply badly injured, in a coma, revived by the cool of the
stone tomb. On Friday, He was confirmed dead, but by Sunday morning,
the tomb was empty. His body had not been stolen. Jesus rose from the
dead and walked from the grave, the same person.

Women were prominent witnesses to Jesus' death, burial, and resurrection. They followed Jesus to Calvary, stood "near the cross" (John 19:25),
watched Jesus die (Matthew 27:55), observed how His body was placed
in the tomb and, before the Sabbath, prepared *spices and perfumes* for His
burial (Luke 23:55-56).

*Then they were the first to find the empty tomb, and the angel instructed them
to tell the "disciples and Peter" that Jesus would meet them in Galilee (Mark
16:1-7). Mary Magdalene was the first to meet and touch the risen Lord; His
second appearance was to other women, with Mary the first to announce the
good news of His resurrection. How did His disciples recognize Him?*

- In His first appearance to Mary Magdalene (Mark 16:9-11;
  John 20:10-18)

- When He met two disciples walking to Emmaus (Mark 16:12-13;
  Luke 24:13-35)

  *The two asked each other, "Were not our hearts burning within us
  while he talked with us on the road and opened the Scriptures?"
  (Luke 24:32). When has your heart burned within, when you
  trusted your risen Lord?*

- Sunday evening, with his disciples (Mark 16:14; Luke 24:33-49; John 20:19-23)

  _____

  _____

- A week later, when Jesus appeared to all eleven disciples (John 20:24-31)

  _____

  _____

- Appearance beside the Sea of Galilee (John 21:1-25)

  Jesus had prepared breakfast on the beach. Three times Peter had denied His Lord and three times Jesus asked, "Do you love me?" (John 21:15-17). When has Jesus restored, reinstated, and reaffirmed your relationship with Him?

  _____

  _____

- On a mountain in Galilee (Matthew 28:16–20)

  We don't know which mountain Jesus chose. But it might have been Mount Arbel with its dramatic views of the entire region from Magdala to Capernaum, Bethsaida to Mount Hermon, and of Gaulanitis (Golan) and Decapolis—"all nations [ethne]" on "the other side." What relational streams do you see from where you are?

  _____

  _____

What are the essentials of this gospel? And what were disciples to do?

- Mark 16:9-16:

  _____

  _____

- 1 Corinthians 15:1-6:

  _____

  _____

- Luke 24:44-48:[7]

  _____

  _____

- Matthew 28:16-20:

_____

_____

PASSIONATE WITNESS TO THE GOOD NEWS—A VIRAL MOVEMENT PRINCIPLE

Commitment to a cause is essential for movements.[8] The disciples had a cause: the resurrection of Jesus validated His uniqueness as the Son of God (Romans 1:1-4). There can be no Kingdom movement without disciples telling and retelling this good news.

What evidence do you have that Jesus Christ is alive?

_____

_____

What does the good news mean to you? And how passionate are you about sharing it?

_____

_____

REFLECTION
What new insights have you gained from this guide?

_____

_____

SHARING
Discuss with your friends who you will share this good news with this week.

_____

_____

"RECEIVE THE SPIRIT"

Invitation Five

ON RESURRECTION SUNDAY EVENING, Jesus visited His disciples. They were not celebrating His resurrection: They did not believe He had risen, and they were frightened of the Jewish leaders responsible for Jesus' death (John 20:19). But He appeared, saying, "Peace be with you!" Repeating this encouragement, Jesus added, "As the Father has sent me, I am sending you"—and, *breathing on* them, He urged, "Receive the Holy Spirit" (John 20:21-22). This was His fifth invitation in disciplemaking.

Having done all necessary for their reconciliation to God, Jesus rose from the grave to commission His disciples to do what He had been doing. Anointed and filled with the Spirit, He cultivated a Kingdom movement of disciplemaking. Now, anointed and filled with the Holy Spirit, His disciples are to do the same: make disciples for God's Kingdom. In this final guide, we review the frames Jesus used, then explore this fifth invitation.

READ

- Matthew 28:16-20; Mark 16:9-20; Luke 24:36-53; Acts 1:1-11
- *Messiah*, chapter 87

REVIEW THE ESSENTIAL FRAMES OF JESUS' MOVEMENT BUILDING

From the preparation phase of Jesus' life, preparing for a life of multiplication:

- _____
- _____
- _____

From the ministry foundation phase, when Jesus modeled multiplication:

- _____
- _____
- _____

From the phase of participation for expanded outreach:

- _____
- _____
- _____

From Jesus' leadership multiplication phase, intentionally focusing on key leaders:

- _____
- _____
- _____

In phase 5 (guides 42–49), we have followed Jesus' final journey, from His entry to Jerusalem to His resurrection and commissioning of His disciples. The focus of His teaching during these final days indicates His priorities. What has been your experience? How have Jesus' final priorities, in His teachings and sacrifice, influenced you?

- Fruitfulness:

_____
_____

- Love:

_____
_____

- Faithfulness:

_____
_____

- The disinherited:

  _____

  _____

- Subversive humility:

  _____

  _____

- Succession to the Holy Spirit:

  _____

  _____

- Sacrifice for others:

  _____

  _____

- Passionate witness to the good news:

  _____

  _____

Has a specific principle from this final phase of Jesus' movement building had a greater impact on you than others? If so, why do you think this was the case?

_____

_____

INVITATION FIVE: "RECEIVE THE SPIRIT"

Jesus was leaving. The time had come. He was handing on His movement: as the Father had sent Him, He was sending His disciples! His ascension, followed by Pentecost, highlighted two essential movement principles:

- *Ascension—letting go!* (Acts 1:7-9)

  What were the risks of trusting disciples—like us—to cultivate His Kingdom?

  _____

  _____

  How well had Jesus prepared for His departure from His movement?

  _____

  _____

Why are such transitions so difficult for most movement leaders to make?

_____

_____

- *Pentecost—the gift!* (Matthew 28:18-20; Mark 16:19-20; Luke 24:49-53; Acts 1:4-8)

    How did Jesus provide continuity for a new era of movement building?

    _____

    _____

    In what way does the Spirit replicate the mission of Jesus in disciples?

    _____

    _____

    What does this tell us about Kingdom-building methods today?

    _____

    _____

Jesus' fifth invitation is "Receive the Spirit." Disciples would be His body to replicate His mission. He took sacrifice to its ultimate end; then, following resurrection, He invited His disciples to be baptized by the same Spirit who baptized Him—for the same work.

HOLY SPIRIT–ANOINTING FOR TRANSITION AND CONTINUITY

The Kingdom of God is not a business corporation or political entity. It is God's way of life, a movement of the Holy Spirit. It is shaped by the Spirit, built on the foundation of God's revelation of Himself in Jesus. It is seen in disciples multiplying disciples; disciples committed to Jesus, the Word, worship, prayer, fellowship, and service.

How did early believers experience the Holy Spirit's presence? And what did His presence signify concerning Jesus (Acts 2:1-47)?

_____

_____

YOUR PLANS

We have come to the end of our journey through the life, disciplemaking, and movement building of Jesus. But, as with the Gospel of Luke, this is only the beginning of a continuing story. Luke's Gospel and Acts are a two-part series. His Gospel tells of Jesus' life and movement building while physically present; in Acts, he recounts the story of the continuing movement cultivated by *His body*—His *church*, believers anointed by the Holy Spirit.

In what ways is your life being changed by this journey in Following Jesus?

_____

_____

What can you share with those you are encouraging as disciples of Jesus?

_____

_____

MOVEMENT EXPANSION—ACTS AND BEYOND!

In Acts, we find the clear missionary strategy of establishing communities that visibly represented the *message* and *methods* of Jesus. These gatherings were called *the body of Christ.*

Read: Acts 1–28—the fifth book of the New Testament and Luke's second letter.

Trace how the movement Jesus started continued to grow.

In what ways did early believers model their mission and movement on Jesus?

_____

_____

How did Jesus' lessons, priorities, values, and example shape their lives and practices?

_____

_____

In what ways did Paul model His ministry and mission on Jesus' model?

_____

_____

APPLICATION FOR TODAY—AND TOMORROW

How can you be part of and grow this kind of community of disciples in your life and context?

_____

_____

Whom could you invite to join you in reading and applying insights from Luke's second letter—Acts—to continue the disciplemaking and movement building that Jesus started?

_____

_____

ACKNOWLEDGMENTS

AS A CHILD, my parents introduced me to biographies of Jesus. My first opportunity to visit the places where He lived came in 1979, with many visits since, including a season at the Jerusalem Study Centre with Dr. William Shea, just a block from the Garden Tomb. Jesus' life became the frame for my life and ministry—for my evangelism and church planting, disciplemaking and movement thinking. Those I could thank are too numerous to name, but . . .

Thanks to many readers for their suggestions, including Rudy Dingjan, Atte Helminen, Pierre Kempf, Stephan Herzog, Dr. Branimir Schubert, Mark Falconer, Simon Martin, and Kaarina Villa, who followed these guides with her weekly discussion groups. Thanks to good friends Maveni Kaufononga, Glenn Townend, Dr. Tony Robinson, and Elkanah Kerosi for their encouragement. And thanks to my pastors, Mau Tuaoi and Hensley Gungadoo, and my local church family at Gilson College Community Church for opportunities to share insights from *Following Jesus*—and for their comments.

Thanks to Bill Hodgson (Power to Change, formerly Campus Crusade for Christ Australia) and John North (Ambassadors for Christ International—Australia), who, six years ago, invited me to cofacilitate SHIFTm2M in Australia—a *process* by which Christian leaders intentionally *shift* from doing ministry to cultivating *movements* by following Jesus' example. Together, we have walked Israel with Steve Hudson (former CEO of Concentric, formerly Global Youth Initiative, USA), Dann Spader (founder of Sonlife), and Mark Edwards (Sonlife Latin America). Mark's *Knowing Him* is an outstanding guide to Jesus' life, which I reference often. I thank these colleagues, who have generously shared their knowledge of Jesus, their love for Him, the land He walked, and how He cultivated His Kingdom movement.

Thanks to Michele Montenegro for giving specific attention to the guides relating to Jesus' women disciples. In April 2015, in the chapel at Magdala beside Galilee, Michele inspired many Christian leaders when she spoke of Jesus' invitations to women.

Thanks to Dr. Reinder Bruinsma for reading a number of drafts and sharing helpful suggestions. A prolific author, Reinder and his wife Aafje have been friends and colleagues for twenty years. Reinder's suggestions have been invaluable.

Thanks to my editor Nathan Brown for his many helpful suggestions, refining and preparing this book for publication—and to the whole team at Signs Publishing for their support. Thanks also to Shane Winfield for the outstanding work he has done with the illustrations.

And thanks also to Judy, for her encouragement—and for her commitment to keeping my feet on the ground!

Peter Roennfeldt
peter@newchurchlife.com

DISCOVER MORE OF *FOLLOWING JESUS* WITH THE *FOLLOWING JESUS* VIDEO SERIES

FILMED ON LOCATION in Israel with Dr. Peter Roennfeldt, these short video clips weave together some of the fascinating historical, cultural, religious, and geographical contexts that were part of the everyday life and world of Jesus. Significant events, locations, and principles from the disciple-making process of Jesus are highlighted, adding further unique insights and detail for believers and seekers today. These can be viewed as you read the Gospels with this book. Use them to enrich your journey—in groups, workshops, or a sermon series on *Following Jesus*.

This video series is available for free viewing and download: www.following-jesus.com

NOTES

EXPERIENCING HIS WORLD
1. Bargil Pixner, *With Jesus through Galilee according to the Fifth Gospel* (Rosh Pina: Corazin, 1992), 15; Peter Walker, *In the Steps of Jesus: An Illustrated Guide to the Places of the Holy Land* (Oxford: Lion Hudson, 2006), 31, suggests a population "as little as 100 people"; and Craig A. Evans, *Jesus and His World: The Archaeological Evidence* (Louisville, KY: Westminster John Knox, 2013), 13, estimates "somewhere between 200 and 400."
2. N. T. Wright, *Simply Jesus: A New Vision of Who He Was, What He Did, and Why He Matters* (New York: HarperCollins, 2011), 176.
3. Rodney Stark, *The Rise of Christianity: A Sociologist Reconsiders History* (New York: HarperOne, 1996), 7, calculates that by the mid-fourth century, 56.5 percent of the population of the Roman Empire—about 34 million—were Christians.
4. Mark Edwards, *Knowing Him: A 50-Day Study in the Life of Christ* (Campus Crusade for Christ Australia, 2010), www.movementbuilders.com.au, identifies five phases: preparation, ministry foundations, ministry training, expanded outreach, and leadership multiplication.
5. R. L. Thomas and S. N. Gundry, *The NIV Harmony of the Gospels* (San Francisco: HarperCollins, 1988); Steven L. Cox and Kendell H. Easley, *Harmony of the Gospels* (Nashville: Holman, 2007).
6. Jerry D. Thomas, *Messiah: A Contemporary Adaptation of the Classic Work on Jesus' Life, the Desire of Ages* (Nampa, ID: Pacific Press, 2002). For a list of other books about Jesus, see https://en.wikipedia.org/wiki/List_of_books_about_Jesus.

PHASE 1: PREPARATION
1. It is not clear that "Mark, the cousin of Barnabas" (Colossians 4:10) is John Mark.
2. Bargil Pixner, *With Jesus in Jerusalem: His First and Last Days in Judea* (Rosh Pina: Corazin, 2005), 11, comments that Mark had probably "heard particulars from the Galilean fisherman Peter." Some surmise that he might have been the young man who fled into the night naked when Jesus was arrested (Mark 14:51-52).

GUIDE 1: JESUS AS A BABY
1. Did Luke interview Mary? Note the references to her point of view: "Mary was greatly troubled . . . and wondered what kind of greeting this might be" (Luke 1:29); "But Mary

treasured up all these things and pondered them in her heart" (Luke 2:19); she "marveled at what was said about him" by Simeon (Luke 2:33); and, after Jesus' experiences at the Feast of Passover when he was twelve, "his mother treasured all these things in her heart" (Luke 2:51).

2. Kenneth E. Bailey, *Jesus Through Middle Eastern Eyes: Cultural Studies in the Gospels* (London: SPCK, 2008), 45, 46.

3. Mark Edwards, *Knowing Him: A 50-Day Study in the Life of Christ* (Campus Crusade for Christ Australia, 2010), 19.

4. Ibid., 20, for these concepts.

5. Leonard Sweet and Frank Viola, *Jesus: A Theography* (Thomas Nelson, 2012), 56, 57: *Katalyma* (inn) was an upper room for guests (compare Luke 22:17), while *pandocheion* (inn) was a rooming house, used of the Samaritan's inn (Luke 10:34).

6. Peter Walker, *In the Steps of Jesus: An Illustrated Guide to the Places of the Holy Land* (Oxford: Lion Hudson, 2006), 22.

7. For a detailed study, see Bailey, op. cit., 25–37.

GUIDE 2: JESUS AS A JEWISH CHILD

1. E. E. Ellis, "Magi" in *The Illustrated Bible Dictionary*, Vol. 2, J. D. Douglas, ed. (Downers Grove, IL: InterVarsity, 1986), 930–31.

2. Pixner, op. cit., 31: "It is not certain whether this ceremony, which is performed today by every 13-year-old boy, was already carried out at the time of the Second Temple period. It seems, however, that a similar custom existed at that time." A Bar Mitzvah celebrated a child becoming "a spiritually responsible person." This is when Jesus spoke His first recorded words (Luke 2:49).

3. Walker, op. cit., 35; Pixner, op. cit., 30–31; Sweet and Viola, op. cit., 88.

4. Robin Ngo, "Monumental Entryway to King Herod's Palace at Herodium Excavated," *Bible History Daily*, December 18, 2014, biblicalarchaeology.org/daily/news/monumental -entryway-to-king-herods-palace-at-herodium-excavated/. For a discussion of possible dates for Herod's death (5, 4, or 1 BC), see Biblical Archaeology Staff, "Herod's Death, Jesus' Birth and a Lunar Eclipse," *Bible History Daily*, July 27, 2021, www.biblicalarchaeology. org/daily/people-cultures-in-the-bible/jesus-historical-jesus/herods- death-jesus-birth-and-a -lunar-eclipse/.

5. Luke 4:16 references a synagogue in Nazareth. Pixner (op. cit., 17) pictures a *mikvah* found beneath Saint Joseph's Church in Nazareth.

6. Craig A. Evans, *Jesus and His World: The Archaeological Evidence* (Louisville, KY: Westminster John Knox, 2013), 13.

7. Pixner, op. cit., 15; Walker, op. cit., 31, suggests a population "as little as 100 people"; Evans, ibid.: "somewhere between 200 and 400."

GUIDE 3: JESUS THE CARPENTER

1. Walker, ibid., 33. For more details, see Pixner, ibid., 34–35.

2. Evans, op. cit., 23–28.

3. See Evans, ibid., 30–33.

4. See Walker, op. cit., 35; Evans, ibid., 28–30.

GUIDE 4: JESUS' COUSIN

1. Walker, ibid., 44–50.

2. Donald McGavran, *The Bridges of God* (New York: Friendship Press, 1981).

3. Sweet and Viola, op. cit., 97.

4. Adapted from Richard Rohr, *The Path of Descent* (Albuquerque: Center for Action and Contemplation, 2014).

PHASE 2: FOUNDATIONS
1. Acronym from *Shift:m2M*, www.movementbuilders.org.au.

GUIDE 5: TRANSITION EXPERIENCES
1. Leonard Sweet and Frank Viola, *Jesus: A Theography* (Nashville: Thomas Nelson, 2012), 113: Jesus' baptism was a revelation, a demonstration of solidarity with us: "He was foreshadowing what he would do on the cross—that is, bear the guilt of humanity."
2. Mark Edwards, *Knowing Him: A 50-Day Study in the Life of Christ* (Campus Crusade for Christ Australia, 2010), 39.
3. Verses taken from Edwards, ibid., 40.

GUIDE 6: "COME AND SEE"
1. Edwards, op. cit., 35.

GUIDE 7: "FOLLOW ME"
1. Peter Walker, *In the Steps of Jesus: An Illustrated Guide to the Places of the Holy Land* (Oxford: Lion Hudson, 2006), 30, 37.
2. Edwards, op. cit., 48, compare Craig A. Evans, *Jesus and His World: The Archaeological Evidence* (Louisville, KY: Westminster John Knox, 2013), 13, 14, with description of Nazareth where no public buildings, paved roads, or mosaics have been found.
3. Michael Frost, *Jesus the Fool: The Mission of the Unconventional Christ* (Peabody, MA: Hendrickson, 2010), 31–36.
4. Ibid., 31–32.
5. Ibid., 33–34.

GUIDE 8: JESUS' RELIANCE ON HOLY SPIRIT POWER
1. Acronym from *Shift:m2M*, www.movementbuilders.org.au.

GUIDE 9: JESUS, THE ONE TEMPLE!
1. Sweet and Viola, op. cit., 66.
2. Steve Chalke and Alan Mann, *The Lost Message of Jesus* (Grand Rapids, MI: Zondervan, 2003), 107.
3. Bargil Pixner, *With Jesus in Jerusalem: His First and Last Days in Judea* (Rosh Pina: Corazin, 2005), 38.
4. Sweet and Viola, op. cit., 173.
5. Chalke and Mann, op. cit., 105. See also Sweet and Viola, op. cit., 171—"healing and sins go together."

GUIDE 10: MEETING NICODEMUS
1. Sweet and Viola, ibid.
2. Chalke and Mann, op. cit., 26–28 for more on this summary.
3. Walker, op. cit., 70–71.
4. Pixner, op. cit., 38–39: The Essenes had not recognized Jonathan, the brother of Judas Maccabee and from a lowly ranking Hasmonean priestly line, when he was enthroned as high priest and king. From that time, they regarded all sacrifices in the temple to be "illegitimate and unclean." It could be that the "many people" who "believed in his name"

because of what He did in the temple included many Essenes, but Jesus "would not entrust himself" to these "extreme zealous followers." He had an entirely different agenda (see John 2:23-25).

GUIDE 11: EXPLOSIVE GROWTH
1. Edwards, op. cit., 56.
2. Ibid., 57.

GUIDE 12: A SAMARITAN WOMAN
1. See Genesis 41:45, 48:1-22, 50:22-26; Joshua 24:1-32; Hebrew 11:22.
2. Mishna Shebiith, 8:10.
3. Kenneth E. Bailey, *Jesus Through Middle Eastern Eyes: Cultural Studies in the Gospels* (London: SPCK, 2008), 201–2.
4. Ibid., 202.
5. Ibid., 214–15.
6. Ellen White, *The Ministry of Healing* (Mountain View, CA: Pacific Press, 1905), 143.

GUIDE 13: A ROYAL OFFICIAL
1. Walker, op. cit., 65–81; Bargil Pixner, *With Jesus through Galilee according to the Fifth Gospel* (Rosh Pina: Corazin, 1992).
2. Walker, ibid., 71.
3. Ibid., 72–73.

GUIDE 15: ON THE MOVE
1. Leonard Sweet and Frank Viola, *Jesus: A Theography* (Nashville: Thomas Nelson, 2012), 129. See also Jonathan L. Reed, *Archaeology and the Galilean Jesus: A Re-examination of the Evidence* (Harrisburg, PA: Trinity Press International, 2002), 149–52.

GUIDE 16: HEALING AT BETHESDA POOL—ON SABBATH!
1. Mark Edwards, *Knowing Him: A 50-Day Study in the Life of Christ* (Campus Crusade for Christ Australia, 2010), 75.
2. Abraham Joshua Heschel, *Shabbat as a Sanctuary in Time* (1951, New York: Farrar, Straus and Giroux, 2005).

GUIDE 18: FISHING WITH JESUS
1. Edwards, op. cit., 83.
2. Ibid., 84.

GUIDE 19: FISHING WITH JESUS
1. Richard A. Horsley and Neil Asher Silberman, *The Message and the Kingdom* (Minneapolis: Fortress, 1997), 1–64, for the social background in this section.
2. Edwards, op. cit., 93.

GUIDE 20: FISHING WITH JESUS
1. Horsley and Silberman, op. cit., 96.
2. Ibid., 26.

GUIDE 21: MORE SABBATH CONTROVERSIES
1. Ibid., 13.

PHASE 4: LEADERSHIP MULTIPLICATION

1. Paulo Cândido de Olivera, "Developing an Interdisciplinary Analysis and Application of Worldview Concepts for Christian Mission" (Andrews University DMin dissertation, unpublished, 2006), 184.
2. For multiple uses of the term *cruciform*—cruciform architecture, DNA, manuscript, melody, and more—see en.wikipedia.org/wiki/Cruciform.

GUIDE 23: A NIGHT IN PRAYER

1. See Richard A. Horsley and Neil Asher Silberman, *The Message and the Kingdom* (Minneapolis: Fortress Press, 1997), 35, 70–71; see also en.wikipedia.org/wiki/Herodians.
2. See en.wikipedia.org/wiki/The_Dirty_Dozen; Leonard Sweet and Frank Viola, *Jesus: A Theography* (Nashville: Thomas Nelson, 2012), 131, quoting Stephen M. Miller, *The Jesus of the Bible* (Uhrichsville, OH: Barbour, 2009), 127.
3. Steve Addison, *Movements that Change the World* (Smyrna, DE: Missional Press, 2009), 11.

GUIDE 24: JESUS' UPSIDE-DOWN GAME PLAN

1. John Stott, *The Message of the Sermon on the Mount* (Downers Grove, IL: InterVarsity, 1978), 15–16.
2. "This affirmed a quality of spirituality that is already present."—Kenneth E. Bailey, *Jesus Through Middle Eastern Eyes: Cultural Studies in the Gospels* (London: SPCK, 2008), 68.
3. Stott, op. cit., 76–81.
4. Steve Chalke and Alan Mann, *The Lost Message of Jesus* (Grand Rapids, MI: Zondervan, 2003), 130–31.
5. Ibid., 132–33.
6. Ibid., 133–34.
7. *Holy Bible: New Living Translation.*
8. Mark Edwards, *Knowing Him: A 50-Day Study in the Life of Christ* (Campus Crusade for Christ Australia, 2010), 112.

GUIDE 25: LEADERSHIP AND AUTHORITY

1. Ibid., 115.

GUIDE 26: LEADERSHIP AND DOUBT

1. Ibid., 118.

GUIDE 27: LEADERSHIP AND GRATITUDE

1. Michael Frost, *Jesus the Fool: The Mission of the Unconventional Christ* (Peabody, MA: Hendrickson, 2010), 97–98.
2. Ibid., 99.
3. Some believe Simon the Pharisee (Luke 7:36-50) and Simon the leper (Matthew 26:6-13; Mark 14:3-9; John 12:2-8) were the same man, reconciling the stories as reports by different witnesses. In these guides, we treat them as different, with the Pharisee living in Galilee and the leper in Bethany. For more comparative details, see guide 45 comments and notes.
4. Unless otherwise credited, see Bailey, op. cit., 239–60, and Frost, op. cit., 99–101, for cultural background.
5. Bailey, op. cit., 242.
6. Nahman Avigad, "Jerusalem Flourishing—A Craft Center for Stone, Pottery, and Glass" in Noah Wiener, ed., *Life in the Ancient World: Crafts, Society and Daily Practice* (Biblical Archaeology Society, 2013), 9, 12-13, 15.

7. Frost, op. cit., 100.
8. Bailey, op. cit., 243–44.
9. Frost, op. cit., 111, describes these as four waves of reality.

GUIDE 29: LEADERSHIP AND MOVEMENT FOUNDATIONS
1. This diagram draws on a number of sources, including Nathan and Kari Shank, *Reproducing Churches Using Simple Tools: "The Four Fields"* (2007). See also Peter Roennfeldt, *Making Disciples Who Multiply: Multiplying Disciples and Multiplying Churches* (2016), 8.

GUIDE 30: LEADERSHIP AND TOUGH ASSIGNMENTS
1. Edwards, op. cit., 125.

GUIDE 31: LEADERSHIP IN TIMES OF CRISIS
1. Chaim Ben David, "Were there 204 Settlements in Galilee at the time of Josephus Flavius?" *Journal of Jewish Studies*, 62, no. 1 (Spring 2011): 21–36; Sweet and Viola, op. cit., 129; Richard A. Horsley, *Galilee: History, Politics, People* (Valley Forge, PA: Trinity Press International, 1995), 190–193.
2. Hershel Shanks, *The Dead Sea Scrolls: Discovery and Meaning* (Biblical Archaeological Society, 2007), 16. Shanks says it is unlikely Luke copied from this manuscript in Luke 1:33-35, but that "they both came out of the same Jewish soil."

GUIDE 32: LEADERSHIP AND DEFECTION
1. Edwards, op. cit., 138.

GUIDE 33: LEADERSHIP AND PREJUDICE
1. Story told by Chalke and Mann, op. cit., 29–30.

GUIDE 34: LEADERSHIP AND THE ROCK
1. See: http://en.wikipedia.org/wiki/Caesarea_Philippi; see also Peter Walker, *In the Steps of Jesus: An Illustrated Guide to the Places of the Holy Land* (Oxford: Lion Hudson, 2010), 93.

GUIDE 35: LEADERSHIP AND TEAM POLITICS
1. For a discussion of emotional triangles, see Jim Herrington, R. Robert Creech, and Trisha Taylor, *The Leader's Journey: Accepting the Call to Personal and Congregational Transformation* (San Francisco: Josey-Bass, 2003), 52–55.

GUIDE 36: WHAT WAS JESUS' IDEA OF CHURCH?
1. For further discussion of a worldview shaped by the crucifixion and in "conformity to the crucified Christ," see Michael J. Gorman, *Cruciformity: Paul's Narrative Spirituality of the Cross* (Grand Rapids, MI: Eerdmans, 2001), 4–7.
2. Robert Banks, *Paul's Idea of Community: The Early House Churches in Their Cultural Setting* (Peabody, MA: Hendrickson, 1994), 27–35.
3. Thomas Kemper, "The *Missio Dei* in Contemporary Context," *International Bulletin of Mission Research*, (October 2014):189, argues that mission begins "in the heart of the Triune God."
4. See Revelation 13:8; Sweet and Viola, op. cit., 12.

GUIDE 37: ESSENTIALS SHARED PLAINLY AND OPENLY

1. R. L. Thomas and S. N. Gundry, *The NIV Harmony of the Gospels* (San Francisco: HarperCollins 1988), 130 (note e), 128 (note b).
2. Bargil Pixner, *With Jesus in Jerusalem: His First and Last Days in Judea* (Rosh Pina: Corazin, 2005), 44–46.
3. "Tabernacles, Feast Of," *The Illustrated Bible Dictionary*, Part 3, ed. J. D. Douglas (InterVarsity, 1980), 1511–12; en.wikipedia.org/wiki/Simchat_Beit_HaShoeivah; compare Ezekiel 47; see also Bargil Pixner, *With Jesus through Galilee according to the Fifth Gospel* (Rosh Pina: Corazin, 1992), 63.
4. Bailey, op. cit., 232–33.
5. Ibid., 234.
6. Ibid., 235.
7. Ibid.
8. Edwards, op. cit., 150.
9. Pixner (2005), op. cit., 50.
10. See Steven L. Cox and Kendell H. Easley, *Harmony of the Gospels* (Nashville: Holman, 2007), xxiv–xxv, and Thomas and Gundry, op. cit., 19–20.
11. Because Essenes disputed the legitimacy of this purification, it was not included in their calendar.
12. "Dedication, Feast Of," *The Illustrated Bible Dictionary*, Part 1, ed. J. D. Douglas (Downers Grove, IL: InterVarsity, 1980), 380; Pixner (2005), op. cit., 52, 53; John 10:22 refers to the timing.

GUIDE 38: THE *PERSON OF PEACE* AND STEPS TO MULTIPLICATION

1. To download free PDF versions of *Planting Churches that Multiply* (2014) by Peter Roennfeldt, a conversation guide to planting new churches, and *New Churches for New People* (2007), go to www.newchurchlife.com/index.php/resources/.
2. Go to www.newchurchlife.com/index.php/resources/ for free PDF versions of this bookmark.

GUIDE 39: JESUS' RADICAL WORLDVIEW AFFIRMED

1. Kenneth E. Bailey, *Finding the Lost* (St. Louis: Concordia, 1992), 97–99; see also Bailey (2008), op. cit., 194–95.

GUIDE 40: JESUS' KEY DISCIPLEMAKING PRINCIPLES AFFIRMED

1. See http://idioms.thefreedictionary.com/let+the+side+down. To "let the side down" is a British and Australian idiomatic expression meaning "to behave in a way that embarrasses or causes problems for a group of people that you are part of."

GUIDE 41: THE LAST COME FIRST

1. Notes on John 11:54 in Thomas and Gundry, op. cit., 157.
2. "Jericho," http://en.wikipedia.org/wiki/Jericho.
3. The first time was in the region of Caesarea Philippi (Matthew 16:21-26; Mark 8:31-37; Luke 9:22-25) and the second after returning from the Mount of Transfiguration to Galilee (Matthew 17:22-23; Mark 9:30-32; Luke 9:43-45).
4. See Pixner (2005), 56–57, for quotations and background in this paragraph.
5. Pixner (2005), 18, 56–57, suggests Lazarus, Martha, and Mary were "apparently celibates," at the time "considered a virtue only for Essenes."

PHASE 5: MOVEMENTS

1. Andrew J. DeJonge, *Giving Up Control: Why Movements Are Preferable to Revivals* (self-published e-book, 2015), 58, 62: The last of the MAWL principles of disciplemaking is to leave—model, assist, watch, and leave.
2. Ibid., 40.

GUIDE 42: FRUITFULNESS

1. Andrew Turner, *Fruitful Church: A Manifesto for Sending* (www.sacredagents.net, 2015), 10: the title of Chapter 1. To "not give a fig" is an idiomatic expression meaning to not care about something or someone.
2. Ibid., 26.
3. Jonathan Sedlek, "More than a Prophet: A Theological Essay on Acts of Mission in Matthew's Gospel" (unpublished manuscript, submitted to the Trinity House Institute in partial fulfillment of MIS501 Holistic Mission, 2014), 3–4.
4. Turner, op. cit., 16, 17.
5. Ibid., 61, back cover.
6. Ibid., 12, 16.

GUIDE 43: LOVE

1. Steve Addison, *Movements That Change the World* (Smyrna, DE: Missional Press, 2009), 11. The others: commitment to a cause, contagious relationships, rapid mobilization, and adaptive methods.

GUIDE 44: FAITHFULNESS

1. See article "Semeion," www.biblestudytools.com/lexicons/greek/nas/semeion.html, meaning a sign, mark, or token by which a person or thing is distinguished from others, recognized, or authenticated.
2. Bargil Pixner, *With Jesus in Jerusalem: His First and Last Days in Judea* (Rosh Pina: Corazin, 2005), 70; see also George R. Knight, *Matthew: The Gospel of the Kingdom*, The Abundant Life Amplifier (Boise, ID: Pacific Press, 1994), 238–39.
3. For three possibilities, see Andy Horvath, "What You Probably Don't Know about 'The Least of These,'" *Christianity Today Weekly Newsletter*, March 6, 2015, www.christianitytoday. com/ct/2015/march-web-only/what-you-probably-dont-know-about-least-of-these.html. Horvath discounts the Jews or the State of Israel as valid possibilities, so this guide focuses on the other two options.
4. For ideas in this section, see Horvath, ibid.

GUIDE 45: THE DISINHERITED

1. For the placement of this meal and the anointing of Jesus in the last week of Jesus' life, see R. L. Thomas and S. N. Gundry, *The NIV Harmony of the Gospels* (San Francisco: HarperCollins 1988), 168 (note).
2. Leviticus 13:45-46; see Pixner, op. cit., 56–57, for background on Bethany being a settlement for lepers.
3. See http://hermeneutics.stackexchange.com/questions/1358/was-jesus-anointed-once-or-twice-on-the-feet-with-perfume for a summary of differences and similarities:

Simon the Pharisee	Simon the Leper
Luke 7:36-50	Matthew 26:6-13; Mark 14:3-9; John 12:1-8
seems to be in Galilee	in Bethany, close to Jerusalem
during Jesus' Galilean ministry, after this the Twelve toured Galilee (Luke 8:1-3)	during His last visit to Jerusalem; the Passover was two days away (Mark 14:1-3)
the perfume: gratitude for forgiveness	the nard ointment: preparation for burial
This Simon did not welcome Jesus with: a kiss washing feet oil on his head	There is no suggestion this Simon neglected to give an appropriate welcome.
Simon the Pharisee was rebuked but the disciples were not rebuked.	Judas and the disciples were rebuked but Simon was not rebuked.

4. Compare Matthew 16:16; see Kenneth E. Bailey, *Jesus Through Middle Eastern Eyes: Cultural Studies in the Gospels* (London: SPCK, 2008), 142–44.
5. See http://en.wikipedia.org/wiki/New_Testament_people_named_Mary for an introduction to the New Testament women named Mary. It is not always clear which person is being identified.
6. Bailey, op. cit., 230: "Here was a woman who got what He was saying."
7. Pixner, op. cit., 82.
8. Ibid., 83.
9. Bailey, op. cit., 222.
10. H. Richard Niebuhr, *The Social Sources of Denominationalism* (New York: Meridian, 1929), 26.

GUIDE 46: SUBVERSIVE HUMILITY

1. Thomas and Gundry, op. cit., 197, commenting on Matthew 26:17; Mark 14:12; and Luke 22:8.
2. Pixner, op. cit., 88.
3. Michael Gorman, *Cruciformity: Paul's Narrative Spirituality of the Cross* (Grand Rapids, MI: Eerdmans, 2001), 4-5; Michael Gorman, *Inhabiting the Cruciform God* (Grand Rapids, MI: Eerdmans, 2009), 1.
4. See "Foot Washing," http://en.wikipedia.org/wiki/Foot_washing: Several Christian denominations—Anglicans, Lutherans, Methodists, Presbyterians, and Roman Catholics—observe the washing of feet on Maundy Thursday of Holy Week; while some—for example, Anabaptists, Seventh-day Adventists, and some Baptists and Pentecostals—practice foot washing as an ordinance, at times called the Ordinance of Humility.
5. Mark Strom, "Paul: Legacy of an Unlikely Radical," in *The Arts of the Wise Leader* (Sydney: Sophos, 2007), 2-3.
6. From the table, Jesus took Passover wine. The word *wine* can signify either fermented or unfermented, but since it was the time when all leaven—a symbol of sin—had been swept from homes, it might be concluded that Passover wine was unfermented.
7. Jerry D. Thomas, *Messiah* (Nampa, ID: Pacific Press, 2003), 354.

8. See Robert Banks, *Paul's Idea of Community: Spirit and Culture in Early House Churches* (Peabody, MA: Hendrickson, 1994), 80–85; compare Robert Banks, *Going to Church in the First Century* (Jacksonville, FL: SeedSowers, 1980), 21–23.
9. Pixner, op. cit., 11.

GUIDE 47: SUCCESSION TO HOLY SPIRIT PRESENCE

1. Richard Rohr, "A Man of Contradictions," *Richard Rohr's Daily Meditations*, Monday, March 30, 2015.
2. Thomas and Gundry, op. cit., 212, commenting on John 18:3.
3. Roland Allen, *The Spontaneous Expansion of the Church: and the Causes Which Hinder It* (London: World Dominion Press, 1949), 8.

GUIDE 48: SACRIFICE FOR OTHERS

1. See "Hematidrosis," http://en.wikipedia.org/wiki/Hematidrosis. This condition is also called hematohidrosis, hemidrosis, or blood sweat.
2. Pixner, op. cit., 124. It can be assumed that Herod Antipas was in Jerusalem for Passover, but there is no indication of where he stayed or where the trial of Jesus took place. Pilate, the governor of Judea, possibly stayed in Herod's Palace—on the western hill, with unhindered views of the city and Temple Mount; Herod Antipas, governor of Galilee and Perea, might have stayed in the Hasmonean Palace, believed to have been closer to the temple; while the Palatial Mansion—also with unhindered views of the temple, now the Wohl Museum—a complex of six luxury homes, with mosaics, mural walls, cisterns, and mikva'ot, was perhaps the High Priest's residence.
3. Gorman (2001), op. cit., 5.
4. Ralph F Wilson, "Seven Last Words of Christ from the Cross," JesusWalk Bible Study Series, www.jesuswalk.com/7-last-words/7_commit.htm#_edn63 (2015): "The word 'spirit' is the common word *pneuma*, 'breathing, breath of life.' It can refer to the Holy Spirit, but here refers to the personal spirit of Jesus, part of the human personality (Hebrews 4:12; 1 Thessalonians 5:23)."
5. N. T. Wright, *Paul: In Fresh Perspective* (Minneapolis: Fortress, 2005), 96.
6. Leonard Sweet and Frank Viola, *Jesus: A Theography* (Nashville: Thomas Nelson, 2012), 101.
7. Ibid., 97.
8. Gorman (2009), op. cit., 1.

GUIDE 49: PASSIONATE WITNESS TO THE GOOD NEWS

1. Jürgen Moltmann, *The Trinity and the Kingdom: The Doctrine of God* (Minneapolis: Fortress, 1993), 76, 77.
2. Ibid., 78. Early manuscripts of Mark's Gospel read: "Why hast thou exposed me to shame?" and "Why hast thou cursed me?"
3. Ibid., 78, 80, for quotations and ideas in this paragraph.
4. For background to both the Church of the Holy Sepulchre and the Garden Tomb, see Peter Walker, *The Weekend that Changed the World: The Mystery of Jerusalem's Empty Tomb* (London: Marshall Pickering, 1999).
5. Pixner, op. cit., 151.
6. Thomas and Gundry, op. cit., 236, note on Matthew 27:63.
7. Paul E. Pierson, *The Dynamics of Christian Mission: History through a Missiological Perspective* (Pasadena, CA: William Carey International University Press, 2009), 21.
8. Addison, op. cit., 55.